The Complete Customer Service Letter Book

CW01637203

The Complete Customer Service Letter Book

Edward W. Werz

Sally Germain

McGraw-Hill, Inc.

New York St. Louis San Francisco Auckland Bogotá
Caracas Lisbon London Madrid Mexico Milan
Montreal New Delhi Paris San Juan São Paulo
Singapore Sydney Tokyo Toronto

The Complete Customer Service Letter Book
International Editions 1993

Exclusive rights by McGraw-Hill Book Co. - Singapore for manufacture and export. This book cannot be re-exported from the country to which it is consigned by McGraw-Hill.

Copyright © 1993 by McGraw-Hill, Inc. All rights reserved. Except as permitted under the United States Copyright Act of 1976, no part of this publication may be reproduced or distributed in any form or by any means, or stored in a data base or retrieval system, without the prior written permission of the publisher.

3 4 5 6 7 8 9 0 SLP UPE 9 8 7 6 5

P/N 069588-1
PART OF
ISBN 0-07-911618-3

Library of Congress Cataloging-in-Publication Data

Werz, Edward W.
The complete customer service letter book / Edward W. Werz. Sally Germain.
p. cm.
Includes index.
ISBN 0-07-069588-1 : -ISBN 0-07-069589-X (pbk.) :
1. Commercial correspondence. 2. Cusotmer service-United States.
I. Germain, Sally. II. Title.
HF5726.W45 1993
651.7'5-dc20 92-36485
CIP

The sponsoring editor for this book was Betsy N. Brown, the editing supervisor was Fred Dahl, and the production supervisor was Pamela Pelton. It was set in Garamond by Inkwell Publishing Services.

When ordering this title, use ISBN 0-07-113771-8

Printed in Singapore

Contents

Preface

The Complete Customer Service Letter Book is a helpful guide to better company-customer communications. This reference book can be used easily and effectively by companies in several ways. We would like to suggest some of its practical applications.

The first is the most obvious—as a guide to writing professional letters that address the many concerns and problems of customers. While some companies have a few prewritten letters available for customer service, most do not. Ironically, the quality of many in-house letters written by employees who are trained in service but not in writing skills may not meet your standards of excellence.

By consulting this guide with nearly 200 model letters, your company's employees can promptly and properly answer your customers' inquiries and needs. And, since the letters are written by customer service experts who are also professional writers, the content and style will present your company in the most professional light.

The extensive "Contents" allows the customer service person to immediately search and find the letter that best serves the purpose. Once the letter is located, it can be easily modified to address the customer's exact situation and the company's particular policy. Each letter includes a helpful description of the reason for it, and is followed by key points to follow in writing a customized response.

A second application for *The Complete Customer Service Letter Book* is as a manual for better customer service. A company can use the letters as a checklist to review its policies and procedures in nearly 200 situations that require attention to customer concerns. While every policy described may not be appropriate for all companies, each offers an example that can open discussion about how your company should handle similar situations.

Third, this guide can be of value as a catalyst to initiate your own program for customer service excellence, including the publication of a Customer Bill of Rights and A Customer Service Policy Manual.

No matter how *The Complete Customer Service Letter Book* is used in your company, you will find its information and suggestions worthwhile. For, in the final analysis, your company is only as strong as your commitment to your customers' satisfaction.

Edward W. Werz
Sally Germain

How to Use the Disk

Your disk of letters from *The Complete Customer Service Letter Book* is organized for your convenience.

Organization

In addition to a Readme file, the disk contains a directory by the name of "Letters."

Within the directory are included all the letters contained in the book (except bonus letters). The filename for each letter is its number in the book. For example, the file named "2.1" contains letter 2.1 (the first letter in Chap. 2 on page 13).

Making a Backup Copy

The disk is a 3.5-in. double-sided, double-density floppy diskette.

You are encouraged to install the contents of the Letters directory on your hard drive, if you have one, and keep the floppy disk as a backup.

To copy the directory onto your hard drive, use the following MS-DOS commands:

```
c:mkdir letters
```

Then:

```
c:copy b:\letters c:\letters
```

If you do not have a hard drive, make a backup copy of the disk, following the appropriate instructions in your system's operator's manual.

Using the Letters in Your Word Processor

The letters have been saved in ASCII (i.e., as text files), so that they can be imported into most or all word processors.

To call a letter up on your screen from the floppy disk or the hard drive, access the directory name, and then type the filename. For example, suppose you want to access letter 2.1 in the book.

For floppy disk users, the pathname is:

```
b:\letters\2.1
```

For hard drive users, it is:

```
c:\letters\2.1
```

If your word processor contains default margins, the letter should appear on the screen with automatic line breaks within those margins.

If your word processor does not contain default margins, the lines of the letter may run off the right edge of the screen. If so, simply define the margins you want, and the line wraps should be adjusted accordingly.

The Complete Customer Service Letter Book

1

What Is Customer Service?

There are many definitions to customer service but our approach is broad and proactive. It includes not only the handling of customer complaints and problems but also any interaction between a company and its customers.

Good customer service includes:

- Providing fast answers to customer inquiries and problems.
- Offering 800 phone numbers, 24-hour service, prompt callbacks and whatever it takes to make doing business with you as easy as possible.
- Friendly, concerned, and responsive people, from the switchboard operator to the shipping department—and everyone in between.
- Making personalized service available whenever possible.
- Backing your product with an ironclad guarantee.
- Delivering more than you promise... every time.
- Showing courtesy, consideration, and concern in all your dealings.
- Being honest, responsible, and reliable.
- Giving customers the best value for their money.

In this decade and into the twenty-first century, the companies that combine these qualities with products that meet their customers' needs will survive and prosper. Companies that lose sight of their customers will disappear.

Establishing a Customer Service Policy for Your Company

Given that a company recognizes the importance of customer service excellence but has not yet implemented a policy, how does it get started?

Initiating a customer service policy requires (1) a commitment to customer service and (2) an understanding of how your customers would like to be served.

Making a commitment to customer service is a companywide decision. But, like all business decisions, its success starts with the company's leadership. Top-level executives must not only verbalize their support, but must back up their commitment with the necessary staff and funding. At first, customer service may seem to be a drain on capital. It is imperative, however, that management realize that in the long run it will pay for itself in customer satisfaction and sales.

Once management has made the commitment, it is their responsibility to educate, motivate and excite every employee to make customer service a priority.

The second part of the customer service formula requires a knowledge and understanding of what the customer really wants. Assumptions are not good enough. While there are many ways of getting this information, the company must talk to its customers. Your efforts here will provide the foundation for your policy. And be prepared for some eye-opening surprises!

To assist you in formulating your customer service policy, a sample manual is offered in the final section of this book. It furnishes many ideas that you can adapt to your own business, as well as sample phrasing of policy.

A Customer Bill of Rights

An innovative approach to committing one's company to customer service excellence is the publication of a Customer Bill of Rights. A Customer Bill of Rights serves two purposes.

First, it summarizes the company's customer service policies for the employees in specific language. By crystallizing your policies on a single sheet of paper, and making that statement an important focal point in the day-to-day running of the business, you make everyone in the company a partner in your pledge to excellence.

Second, by communicating the Bill of Rights to customers, you tell them that they are dealing with a company that has made their satisfaction a priority. It is not only good public relations, it also clarifies exactly what a customer can expect. As a confidence-builder, a Customer Bill of Rights is unequalled in its ability to reassure buyers that they can count on your word.

How to Create a Customer Bill of Rights for Your Company

Because the Customer Bill of Rights is created for both employees and customers, ideally they should both have input in its creation. The first step is to survey customers to determine the policies they consider of prime importance. This can be done by means of three methods:

- A survey letter.
- Telemarketing.
- Focus groups.

Once collected, the information should then be summarized and made available to all employees. After reviewing the customer feedback, employees submit their own recommendations to management, and a staff committee is set up to turn all the data into a final statement of policy.

Once accepted by top management and the committee, the policy should be enthusiastically launched. A company might organize a special event such as a picnic, a talent show, or a breakfast to publicly announce the final Customer Bill of Rights to all employees. The document should be announced in a special way to customers too: announced in the customer newsletter, printed in product brochures, or inserted in all product shipments.

Every year, a committee should review the Customer Bill of Rights and modify it to reflect any changes in the needs of customers and the company.

Figures 1.1 and 1.2 are two examples of a Customer Bill of Rights currently in use. Each of these companies is not only a leader in its field but is known and respected for its dedication to customer care. The Quill Corporation is a leading direct marketing supplier of office supplies and equipment. The Quill Customers' Bill of Rights is an excellent example of a policy that espouses the principles of general customer care and could be a model for any company that makes this commitment. On the other hand, the Anchor Computer, Inc. Customers' Bill of Rights was formulated specifically to address the concerns of computer service bureau customers.

Whether it is very specific or general in nature, your company's bill of rights should be decided by the nature of your business and the actual concerns of your customers.

THE QUILL CUSTOMERS'

BILL OF RIGHTS

Restated and approved at Lincolnshire, Illinois, on Monday the First of May, One Thousand Nine Hundred and Eighty-nine.

The undersigned officers and the more than 1100 employees of Quill Corporation express a desire to clearly state the principles and ideals which guide all of us at Quill in our relationship with our customers.

We feel this unusual step is necessary at this time because we find ourselves, when we are customers...both as individuals and as a company.. frequently dissatisfied with the way we are treated. Lack of interest, discourteousness, bad service, late deliveries and just plain bad manners are too common.

We can't tell others how to run their businesses (except by not buying from them). But we can and will run Quill as we feel a business should be run. Therefore, the following is a list of what we consider to be the inalienable rights of our customers. *We expect to be held to account whenever we deny any of these rights to any customer:*

1. As a customer, you are entitled to be treated like a real, individual, feeling human being...with friendliness, honesty and respect.
2. As a customer, you are entitled to full value for your money. When you buy a product, you should feel assured that it was a good buy and that the product is exactly as it was represented to be.
3. As a customer, you are entitled to a *complete* guarantee of satisfaction. This is especially true when you buy the product sight unseen through the mail or over the phone.
4. As a customer, you are entitled to fast delivery. Unless otherwise indicated, the product should be shipped within 8-32 hours. In the event of a delay, you are entitled to immediate notification, along with an honest estimate of the expected shipping date.
5. As a customer, you are entitled to speedy, courteous, knowledgeable answers on inquiries. You are entitled to all the help we can give in finding exactly the product or information you need.
6. As a customer, you are entitled to the privilege of being an individual and dealing with individuals. If there is a question on your account, you are entitled to talk with or correspond with another individual so the question can be resolved immediately on the most mutually satisfactory basis possible.
7. AS A CUSTOMER, YOU ARE ENTITLED TO BE TREATED EXACTLY AS WE WANT TO BE TREATED WHEN WE ARE SOMEONE ELSE'S CUSTOMER.

Jack Miller *President* | Harvey L. Miller *Secretary* | Arnold Miller *Treasurer*

COPYRIGHT 1970, QUILL CORPORATION

Figure 1.1. The Quill Corporation Customers' Bill of Rights.

Customer's Bill of Rights

- You have the right to have your job delivered on time, every time.
- You have the right to know how your job is being processed, what stage it is in and when it will be finished.
- You have the right to be treated courteously and to have questions answered and information given promptly.
- You have the right to ask us to advise you on the way to run your job.
- You have the right to expect cost-justified enhancements.
- You have the right to be confident that we use the best software.
- You have the right to receive comprehensive reports that are easy to understand - before your job is mailed, each and every time.
- You have the right to see sample names from each and every list you rent.
- You have the right to have real duplicates identified and reported to you, each time, every time.
- You have the right to use merge/purge data for sophisticated response analysis programs.
- You have the right to discuss your job with top management.

"If your rights are violated, I want to know about it!"

Len Schenker, President

Figure 1.2. The Anchor Computer, Inc. Customers' Bill of Rights.

What Makes a Good Customer Service Letter?

Well-executed customer service letters have five important characteristics in common:

1. They are *responsive.*

The letter answers the customer's inquiry or problem. Too frequently, companies rely on a handful of letters to answer all situations. A letter that does not show that you understand the customer's problem will only cause more harm than good.

2. They are *empathetic.*

The customer needs to know that you relate to the frustration and/or inconvenience the customer has experienced on a human level. By showing empathy, you help defuse the customer's anger and build rapport.

3. They are *personal.*

Forget about photocopied form letters if you want to keep and satisfy customers. Letters should be individually typed and signed. The letter should be written by a person in the company—not sent from a department. And, most importantly, a person-to-person dialogue must be established between the company representative and the customer. Always include the writer's direct phone number.

4. They are *concise* and *easy to understand.*

Explain the company's position in as few words as possible. Don't get into long-winded explanations. Tell the customer what you can do and exactly what the customer must do next. Use clear language to eliminate any misunderstandings

5. They use a *friendly, relationship-building tone.*

You're writing to a customer—your most valuable asset. Tell customers they are special and that you want them to be happy. Avoid cold, legal-sounding language.

By remembering these five guidelines, you'll write outstanding customer service letters that not only solve problems, but further the possibility of future business.

Two sample letters follow. The first is a typical example of the badly written letters currently used by a majority of companies. The second is written with an understanding of the principles outlined above and of the power of positive customer communications.

Sample of a Bad Letter

Situation Too often, companies announce an internal policy or procedural decision to customers without concern for how it affects the customer's business. In this instance, a "proclamation" is made without explanation or without offering ways to help the customer function during the shutdown. The impersonal tone is also an example of the vendor's indifference. It is this type of letter that *The Complete Customer Service Letter Book* helps to eliminate from contemporary business practice.

The Letter To Whom It May Concern:

Adams Truck Supply will be closed from 8/13 to 8/29.

If you are planning to place an order, please do so by 8/3. Orders placed up to that date will be shipped before the closedown. Orders placed after that date will be held until the first week in September for processing.

Please pass this notice to all parties who need to know.

Thank You.

Adams Truck Supply

Key Points

- This impersonal letter does not address the customer by name. In addition, it is not signed by an individual.
- No explanation of the reason for the shutdown is offered. This tells customers that they are not held in high enough esteem to deserve an explanation.
- The customer's needs are not taken into consideration.
- The customer is not told what to do if the shutdown will cause hardship.

Sample of a Good Letter

Situation The following is an example of a strong and effective customer service letter. Dan Abramson of G & G Catering has sent Stevenson Food Distributors an order for 300 pounds of new potatoes. The order required delivery by 11/1. Because of an error, Stevenson delivered the potatoes two days after they were needed. G & G was furious and told Stevenson that they would use a different supplier in the future. Stevenson's sales manager writes this letter to try to save the account.

The Letter Dear Mr. Adamson:

As the sales manager of Stevenson Food Distributors, I wanted to personally write you to apologize for the error we made.

You ordered 100 lbs. of new potatoes on 10/25 and specified that the order was needed on or before 11/1. We accepted the order but did not meet your delivery requirement.

There is no excuse for Stevenson missing the date. If we couldn't meet it, we should have notified you in advance. Your ability to serve your customers was put in jeopardy. For that, we are truly sorry.

You have been a loyal customer for over three years. In that time, we have met your delivery dates on time . . . until this incident. Won't you give us another chance? We value your business and will do everything in our power to ensure that you receive the quality, on-time service you deserve.

I will call you next week to see what I can do to make up for this unfortunate error.

Sincerely,

Roger Moss

Key Points

- Be personal but professional in identifying yourself and explaining the reason for your letter.
- Restate the problem.
- Be empathetic by acknowledging the customer's right to be angry. Make your concern for what is important to your customer clear when you apologize for your mistake.
- State that you appreciate and want the customer's business.
- Remind the customer of your successful relationship until now.
- Explain what you will do next.

2

Introductory and Announcement Letters

First impressions count! The first time that you make contact with a customer about any new service, product, or announcement is a unique opportunity to set the groundwork for a strong and long-lasting relationship.

The tone of introductory and announcement letters is especially important because you are making contact with your customers at a time when you are not directly trying to make a sale. The fact that your communication provides information that will be of interest or assistance creates an unpressured exchange. Here's a chance to reinforce the fact that you have an existing relationship with your customer—a relationship that is very important to you.

Write to the customer as you would to a friend with good news. A positive, upbeat letter makes a favorable impression. When possible, recognize the customer as such in your letter. Try to make the customer feel special. Everyone appreciates recognition, and this is a favorable time to express it. If appropriate, use your knowledge about the customer's needs, interests, and concerns. Personalized letters produce far more attention and interest.

Keep the following key points in mind when writing introductory and announcement letters:

Key Points

- An introductory letter should be friendly in tone without being overly casual.
- Acknowledge that you are aware the customer is a customer. Whenever possible, reinforce that relationship.
- Point out the benefits of your announcement in terms the customer will understand and appreciate. Use personal references to the customer's concerns and interests, when doing so is appropriate.
- Clearly explain to the customer what action should be taken. Be specific, if you can, about when something will take place. Dates and times should be included.
- Thank the customer for past patronage.

2.1 Introducing a New Customer Service Representative

Situation Jim Stevens, one of Allied Industries' customer service reps, has left the company. Sara Kerner has been appointed to replace Jim. Notification must be made to an important customer.

The Letter Dear ______:

As you may have heard, Jim Stevens, your customer service representative has left Allied Industries to further his education. Jim was one of our best customer service representatives and we will miss him.

We are writing to announce the appointment of Sara Kerner as your new customer service representative. Sara has been with us for five years and is assigned to important national accounts such as yours. She has been honored as employee of the month on four separate occasions. We are confident that you will find Sara as professional and responsive to your company's special needs as Jim has been. Sara will be calling you in a few days to arrange an introductory meeting. We want to ensure that you continue to receive attentive service without interruption.

Finally, I'd like to take this opportunity to tell you that we appreciate your business and to say thank you. Please do not hesitate to call me if you have any questions or if I can be of further assistance.

Sincerely,

Tom Peterson
Sales Manager

Key Points

- Inform the customer of the reason for the change. Say something positive about the representative who has left.
- Announce the new appointee. Make sure to state his/her credentials. Explain the new rep's credentials, if possible.
- Tell the customer what will happen next. Do not leave room for doubt about the continuation of your excellent service.
- Restate how important the customer is to you and your business.

2.2 Announcing a New Product/Product Line

Situation Royal Packaging has developed a new product line. A letter is being sent to all customers describing its features and benefits.

The Letter Dear ______:

The Royal Packaging Company is happy to announce its Environment Line of shipping envelopes constructed from 100 percent recyclable corrugated paperboard.

Like you, Royal Paper is concerned about the future of the environment. Because we are committed to its preservation, we're leading the packaging industry with the introduction of this innovative, environmentally sound product line.

The Environment Line provides you with the same quality envelope that you have been using and, at the same time, limits the destruction of our national forests. It features 48 different sized shipping envelopes to meet your exact needs. Custom sizes are available by quotation.

We've enclosed our catalog and price list. You'll notice that you can help the environment and still purchase at truly competitive prices.

Your sales representative will call you next week to discuss this exciting product line.

Sincerely,

Lois Cruthers
Sales Manager

P.S.: If you'd like to place an order now, call us at 1-800-555-5555.

Key Points

- Describe the new product. Detail how the customer will benefit.
- When possible, describe the features that show the product line's quality and reliability.
- Mention what has been enclosed with the letter.
- Tell the reader what to expect next from your company.
- Add a final sales message in the P.S.

2.3 Announcing a Sale

Situation Chelsie's Department Store wants to offer its best customers a special buying opportunity. This letter announces an invitation to a customers-only sale.

The Letter Dear ______:

This letter is being sent to our best customers only!

For years you've been a frequent customer of Chelsie's. Your loyal patronage has been noticed and we'd like to show our appreciation.

Announcing "Best Customer Nights" by invitation only. Once a month, we're opening our doors for an after-hours sale—exclusively for our best customers.

And that's you!

You're invited to a fun-filled evening of refreshments, fashions, and savings.

Plus, a fabulous Spring fashion show. You'll get a sneak preview of all the new styles—before anyone else—and when your size and favorite color are available.

Best of all, you'll save money with our "best customer discounts."

The fun begins at 7:00 P.M. on July 10. We've made a reservation in your name.

Sincerely,

Joan Nickells
Store Manager

P.S.: Wait until you visit our dazzling dessert and coffee buffet!

Key Points

- Let the customer know that he/she is special.
- When possible, announce the sale in a manner that adds value to the event.
- Describe the benefits of attending.
- Give the reader an incentive to participate.
- Provide an additional benefit in the P.S.

2.4 Announcing a Change of Address

Situation Shuman Printing, Inc. is moving to a new location and it will be closed for three weeks during the move. Customers must be notified well in advance of the move.

The Letter Dear ______:

Shuman Printing is pleased to announce a move to a new, larger facility. Our new plant and offices will now be located at 222 W. Houston Ave., in Ridgefield Connecticut. The new telephone number is 203-555-2222.

We have planned our move carefully to ensure that your work will not be interrupted. We will close from September 13 through the end of the month. During the move, our Stanford location will be operating at full production. If you planned to print in Ridgefield during this period, your job will be rescheduled to Stanford. There will be no interruption of service. As of October 1, our new plant will be able to handle all your printing needs.

In fact, our Ridgefield facility expands our production capabilities by over 50 percent. And, our new, state-of-the-art, eight-station web offset press, with an on-line sheeter and folder, will enable us to handle a wider variety of large-run, multicolor jobs.

Once the plant is open, we will invite you for a VIP tour. In case you need to speak with us during the transition from September 13-30, we can be reached at 203-555-5555.

We appreciate your patience during this exciting expansion.

Sincerely,

Ralph Durant
Plant Manager

Key Points

- Explain your move.
- Provide customers with your new address, phone number, and special instructions regarding service during the move.
- Use this opportunity to promote new equipment, larger facilities, etc.
- Offer your customers a chance to visit your new plant/office.
- Reassure the customer by offering a special phone number and/or contact person to handle questions during the move.

2.5 Announcing New Hours

Situation A letter is being sent to the Lumber Warehouse customer list announcing expanded hours.

The Letter Dear ______:

Due to customer demand, the Lumber Warehouse is happy to announce expanded hours on weekdays and Saturday.

Our new hours are 7:00 A.M. to 10:00 P.M. Monday through Friday and 7:00 A.M. through 7:00 P.M. on Saturdays. These new hours should make it even more convenient to shop at Lumber Warehouse in the future.

As always, our warehouse staff will be available to help you load your vehicle with construction materials. There is no charge for this service.

We look forward to serving you during these new hours.

Sincerely,

Donna Stone
Store Manager

Key Points

- Explain the new hours.
- Suggest how the customer will benefit.
- Promote another loyalty-building service.
- Close with a positive statement.

2.6 Announcing New Management

Situation A change in management at Precision Engineering has taken place. A letter is being sent to notify customers of that change.

The Letter Dear ______:

Because of the long-time relationship between our two companies, we'd like you to be among the first to know about an important change in management at Precision Engineering, Inc.

John Waltham, our Vice President of Manufacturing, has retired after 27 years of noteworthy service.

We are happy to announce that Jim Newhouse has been appointed to succeed John as Vice President. Jim has been with Precision for over 11 years as Operations Manager. His experience, knowledge, and professionalism make Jim the ideal person to tackle this challenging position.

We are sure that you'll find Jim to be responsive to the needs of your company.

Sincerely,

Judith Kramer
President

Key Points

- State the change in management, and offer some background information about the new staff member.
- Explain how the change will benefit the customer.
- Close with your expectations that the customer will be satisfied with this change.

2.7 Announcing the Sale of a Company Division

Situation Trusty Toys, Inc. has sold a division of the company. Notice of this change must be sent to customers.

The Letter Dear ______:

Trusty Toys, Inc. announces the sale of its Fluffy Bears division to Consolidated Novelties. The sale was completed on March 12.

With the sale of this division, all Trusty Toys' companies and divisions will be engaged in developing and marketing high-tech, electronic toys and hobby products. Our focus will again be directed toward the products that have made us the industry leader.

If you wish to continue doing business with Fluffy Bears, you can contact Consolidated Novelties at 222 N. Greer St., Denver, Colorado 80202.

We hope this change does not inconvenience you. If you have open orders, they will be fulfilled by Trusty Toys within the next two weeks. Thereafter, Consolidated Novelties will handle all Fluffy Bears business directly.

Thank you for your past patronage. Trusty Toys looks forward to serving you in the future with the most advanced electronic toys available.

Sincerely,

Heather Davis

Chief Financial Officer

Key Points

- Announce the sale of the division.
- Explain how the sale will benefit the customer.
- Provide information for customers who wish to continue doing business with the old division.
- Offer thanks for past business.

2.8 Announcing the Discontinuance of a Service

Situation Handy Direct Mail Services, Inc. has realized that a service offered to its customers has been underused. The company can no longer afford to offer the service and must contact its customers to inform them of this change. A new brochure will be enclosed to replace the old one that listed the now discontinued service.

The Letter Dear ______:

We are writing to inform you that as of February 10 we will no longer offer custom hand assembly. Over the past year, our customers have requested less and less of this specialized service. Because of this decrease in demand, we cannot maintain our crew of hand laborers.

If you need this service in the future, we recommend that you contact Made By Hand, Inc. at 222 Stillwell Ave., Dayton, Ohio 45401.

As you know, HDMS is a full-service direct mail and print promotion company. We continue to offer an integrated array of computer, mailing, printing, fulfillment, and creative services. HDMS provides expert direct mail advice and guidance to customers to help them save money while achieving their marketing objectives.

We've enclosed a brochure which outlines the services that are available at Handy Direct Mail Services, Inc.

We look forward to working with you on your next project.

Sincerely,

Bill Atkins
President

Key Points

- Describe the service that is being discontinued.
- Explain the reason for this change.
- Offer the customer an alternative to this service or another vendor that provides it.
- Use this opportunity to state which services you still offer. Thank the customer for their continued business.

2.9 Announcing a Facility Closing

Situation After many rumors, Barco International has announced to the press that it will be moving its Tallahassee, Florida operation to a new facility under construction in Panama City. The company has decided to send a letter formally announcing this development to all customers. In addition, Barco wants to announce that steps have been taken to ensure that the move will run smoothly and that any difficulties encountered will be handled by the company.

The Letter

Dear ______:

As you may have read in the newspaper, Barco International will close its Tallahassee, Florida components plant on June 22.

The closing of the Tallahassee operation will mark an important turning point for Barco and its customers. The Tallahassee plant is being closed so that a newer, larger, completely computerized operation will open in Panama City. The new plant will increase our capacity threefold and enable us to provide warehouse space so that we can hold your inventory until you need it.

Our new Panama City plant will open on April 22, sixty days before the closing of our Tallahassee operation.

All inquiries, orders, or correspondence should therefore be forwarded to Panama City as of April 22.

Barco has established an Office of Transition to ensure that you continue to receive the excellent service that you have learned to expect. A special phone number has been installed to handle any questions or special requests. Call 555-5555 if you need assistance.

We hope that our plant closing does not cause you any hardships. We know that our new facility will make us better prepared to meet your future needs.

Sincerely,

Alex Carson
General Manager

Key Points

- Announce the closing and provide the date.
- Explain the reason for the closing and offer related benefits, if possible.
- Describe how problems will be dealt with.
- Close with an optimistic statement about the future of the company and its relationship with the customer.

2.10 Announcing Consolidation of Locations

Situation Jeffrey Containers is about to move their operations to a single location. Customers must be informed of the consolidation, and the following letter is sent out.

The Letter Dear ______:

As you know, Jeffrey Containers operates two distribution facilities in New York City. We will be consolidating these operations as of November 23. From that date, all business will be conducted from the East 9th Street location. The West 36th Street warehouse will be closed.

We believe that this consolidation will eliminate confusion while concentrating our resources for a more efficient and productive operation.

We've already ordered a new computer system and have begun to redesign the layout of the 9th Street warehouse. In addition, we will shortly be installing a fully automated picking system. All these improvements will result in accurate, on-time delivery of your orders.

Jeffrey Containers has always made excellence in customer service our number-one priority. The changes described will help us continue to make that goal a reality.

Sincerely,

Larry Jeffrey
President

Key Points

- Describe the consolidation.
- Explain the reason for the change. Tell customers how they will benefit.
- When possible, provide additional reasons why the consolidation will help customers.
- Close by restating your dedication to customer service.

2.11 Announcing a Company Contest

Situation Giveaway Promotions, Inc. has decided to run a contest for its customers. The objective of the contest is to build customer goodwill and keep Giveaway Promotion's name prominent in the customer's mind. A letter is being sent to all customers announcing the contest and explaining the rules.

The Letter

WIN A TRIP FOR TWO TO PARIS!

Dear ______:

Yes, it's true! Giveaway Promotions, Inc. would like to send you, our valued customer, and a guest of your choice away for an unforgettable week in romantic Paris, France. You'll fly first class, stay in the finest hotels and eat in four-star restaurants.

How do you win? It's easy! Just send us the answer to the following question by September 1. Our panel of judges will choose the most creative answer as our winner. If you win, you'll be immediately notified.

Here's the question:
What is the most creative way you have used a Giveaway Promotions' product to build your business?

Please type or write your answer on an 8½ × 11-inch sheet of paper and mail it to Giveaway Promotions, Inc. Customer Contest #1, 454 Ellison Rd., Ste. D, Phoenix, AZ 85021. Be sure to include your name, business, address, and phone number.

This contest is another way in which we say, "We appreciate your business."

Wouldn't you like to spend seven days in Paris this fall? Send us your answer today. You can't win . . . if you're not in!

Sincerely,

Jane Ash
V.P. Marketing

P.S.: Dinner at Maxim's? Of Course!

Key Points

- Announce the contest in a bold, exciting manner.
- Describe the winning prize(s).
- Tell the customer exactly how to enter and what to do next.
- Offer thanks to customers for their past patronage.
- Use a P.S. to draw attention to the contest and its prize.

2.12 Announcing Company Involvement in Community Activity

Situation Smith, Rosen, and Collingswood Associates is sponsoring a community fair that will help raise funds for academic scholarships for local students. A letter is being sent to customers, employees, and friends to invite them to attend.

The Letter Dear ______:

January 15 marks the seventh anniversary of the Wildwood Senior High School Fair. We are proud that Smith, Rosen, and Collingwood Associates is again a corporate sponsor of this worthwhile fundraiser. Our involvement represents another example of our commitment to the community in which we live and work.

Every year, the Wildwood Fair brings out thousands of community residents for wholesome family fun. Besides the games, rides, and contests, the fair boasts the best home cooking to be found in the county. The popular bake-off and western barbecue are always highlights.

This year, all revenues will be used to support the Senior Scholarship Fund. The scholarship fund provides financial aid to Wildwood students with excellent high school academic records. Without this help, many students would be unable to further their education.

Smith, Rosen, and Collingwood invites you to bring your family and friends to this year's event. Your participation is what will help make it a success.

So, come on out! Enjoy the day and help support a wonderful group of deserving students.

Sincerely,

Dan Smith
Senior Partner

P.S.: There's a free tee shirt waiting for you at the ring toss booth. I look forward to seeing you there.

Key Points

- Announce the event, its time, and the place.
- Promote the event by describing the activities or program.
- Explain why your company is supporting this community activity.
- Ask your customers, employees, and friends to attend.

3

Letters Answering Inquiries

Despite the use of 800 or free phone numbers, to make calling in orders or inquiries easier, many customers still use the traditional letter to request information from your company. Your responses to these inquiries always offer you excellent opportunities to make a positive impression on your customers while providing the information requested.

The promptness and manner of your response say a great deal to customers about what kind of company you are. If you are slow to get back to them, will you show similar disinterest in them as customers? If your response letter is poorly written or sloppily presented, can they trust the quality of your products or services? If you appear to hedge your answers to their questions or concerns now, how interested are you really in them, their company, and its needs?

On the other hand, if your response sounds and looks professional, is received in a timely manner, shows an interest in the customer's questions and concerns, as well as a sincere desire to work with them, you've scored a plus for yourselves in customers' minds.

Even if you do respond promptly, inquirers may no longer remember the specifics of their letters to you, or recall that they wrote at all. It is always a good idea to review the customer's request right at the beginning of your response, or include the actual letter if possible.

An inquiry response letter may also give you the chance to educate your customer about the products and services offered by your company that are of greatest interest to the reader. In a subtle way, you can often point out a product or service feature and describe how it will benefit your customer. Because the focus of your response is to inform, any sales effort within your response should be presented casually, or even as an afterthought.

Since a letter is a personal communication between two individuals, remember to use every customer communication as an opportunity to project your company's image in the way you wish. Remember that an inquiry response letter is a special chance to have personal contact with your customer, both at their initiation and without the specific pressure of an impending sale. Use this chance to develop and reinforce your relationship with the buyer.

Customers like to know they are appreciated and that suppliers have their interests at heart. Remember to let your customers know that you care.

Key Points

- Restate what the inquiry is about. Even if your reply is prompt, the customer may no longer remember the specifics of the original request. You may want to actually return the customer's original letter with your response.
- Make sure that your communication conveys the image of the company that you wish to project. Avoid sloppy, photocopied price lists or impersonal form letters.
- Remind the inquirer that you are aware of their customer status.
- Use the opportunity to promote a sale, a special, or another point you want to bring up—something that goes beyond their inquiry.
- Use every inquiry to build rapport with your customer.
- Show the inquirer how convenient it is to order, how easy you are to work with, and so on.

3.1 Answering a Request for Current Pricing

Situation Smythe Corporation is a manufacturer of wastebaskets for the home and office. They sell to consumer houseware stores and office furnishings suppliers. Ann Harper, the buyer for Homedeco, a large home furnishings store, has requested a current price list. A price increase is scheduled for the following month, but the account rep responding to Ms. Harper's request will want to cushion this information with some sort of positive news, a special offer, or other benefits of doing business with Smythe.

The Letter Dear Ms. Harper:

Thank you for requesting our current price list.

Your timing is perfect to reorder, since the price increase you were notified about in January is scheduled for April 29—a month from Friday.

To assist you, I've taken the liberty of marking in red the items you've ordered in the past. And, if you decide to order at least three new style numbers along with a minimum of 2 dozen of any of our basic items, you'll qualify for a special discount.

Since Smythe Corp. plans to continue this special offer after the increase goes into effect, almost all your additional costs should be offset if you're able to stock that quantity of merchandise.

When you've had a chance to review the numbers, I'd be happy to work with you to come up with the most cost-effective plan for Homedeco. I will call you next week to see if you're ready to discuss this further.

Your interest in Smythe Corporation is always appreciated.

Sincerely

Key Points

- Thank the customer for their inquiry.
- Make a special offer the customer can take advantage of or remind them of the benefits of using your company.
- Show that you have the customer's interests in mind.
- Explain specifically what will happen next.
- Let your customer know that you appreciate them.

3.2 Answering a Request for Inventory Information

Situation A manufacturer of shipping cartons has received a customer inquiry requesting stock levels of several items, but the customer has not specified the quantities that will be needed or when they will be needed. To respond, the sales department wants to provide the information requested while reminding the customer that product availability might change. The response letter should also mention that the supplier will try to be flexible in order to meet the customer's needs.

The Letter Dear Mr. Hopkins:

We appreciate your request for Boxmaster's current inventory on Stock Numbers 0046 through 0079. Although we ran the enclosed stock report as soon as your letter arrived in the Order Department, you may want to call and confirm that these counts have not changed significantly prior to sending in your next order.

With a four-week lead time for production, we can supply you with any quantity needed of our entire line of standard items. If you anticipate needing an exceptionally large number of pieces, or a shorter delivery time, we'll do everything possible to work with you.

I went ahead and checked the stock numbers you order most frequently. Based on your recent buying history, we should have adequate stock on hand to ship any of those items.

Thank you for contacting us. It's always our pleasure to serve you.

Sincerely,

Sales Department

Key Points

- Tell customers you appreciate their request and what information you have enclosed in response. Point out that you are responding promptly.
- Show your willingness to meet the customer's needs, and position yourself as their business "partner."
- Reinforce your existing relationship by including information specific to their account.
- Close in a friendly manner.

3.3 Answering an Inquiry on Credit Policy

Situation A new customer, while placing an opening order, has asked about establishing an open line of credit. A letter must be sent out in response.

The Letter Dear ______:

We were very pleased to receive your opening order, P.O. #6483. In response to your inquiry about our credit policy, we will be happy to establish a line of credit on your behalf following our receipt of these credentials:

D & B Rating Report.
One (1) bank reference.
Three (3) trade references.

I've enclosed the forms we'd like used for this purpose.

Assuming you are approved, your opening line of credit would not exceed $10,000. Generally speaking, we require four weeks of processing time before you can be established as an open account customer.

In the meantime, we can fulfill your current order on a COD or prepaid basis. I hope this will not cause you any inconvenience. Long term, we have found that this policy works best for us to supply you on an immediate delivery basis.

Please let us know as soon as possible how we should handle your order #6483. While we are waiting to hear from you, we will begin to assemble your order and begin preliminary processing to open your account.

I would again like to thank you for choosing us for your needs. We look forward to a long and mutually beneficial relationship between our companies.

Sincerely,

Vice President, Finance

Key Points

- Thank your new customer for the order. Acknowledge the credit inquiry.
- State your company's policy as simply and impersonally as possible.
- Add any additional information required to answer the customer's questions.
- Explain what your policy would mean in terms of the customer's next action and yours.
- Thank the customer again for their patronage and express your expectations for future business.

3.4 Answering a Request for Available Locations

Situation In response to a customer's request for available locations, Harris Sports Centers goes beyond providing the basic information by making these locations sound attractive to the customer. Convenience, special staffing, a free visit or tour, accessible parking, or transportation are just a few of the customer benefits that can be pointed out, along with a list of addresses.

The Letter Dear Ms. Johnson:

Welcome to Harrisville! We were very pleased to hear about your recent move and that you're considering joining one of our Harris Sports Centers. I've enclosed a list of all centers in the Harrisville area, as you requested, plus the hours for each.

You may be interested in knowing that, as a Harris Sports Centers member, you will be entitled to use the facilities at any of our Centers. While your membership will be affiliated with one location in particular, an advance phone call will sign you up for any one of seven daily exercise classes in any of our five locations.

If you prefer to use our weight training facilities, lifecycles, treadmills, stairmasters, rowing machines, pools, or other equipment, no advance phone call is necessary. Just show up with a Harris Sports Centers membership card and you'll be given entry.

Any of our Harris representatives would be happy to show you around if you'd like to stop by for a tour—or a trial workout or class—and no advance notice is necessary.

You may have already heard that Harris is considered a state-of-the-art exercise facility with the friendliest, most accommodating staff in the area. It's the next best thing to having a staff of personal trainers with all the equipment you might want right at home.

We hope you'll give us a call and see for yourself!

Sincerely,

General Manager

P.S.: I forgot to mention our fabulous snack bar—healthy, delicious, and reasonably priced breakfast, lunch, and snack foods to top off a satisfying workout!

Key Points

- Extend a warm, friendly introduction. Let the reader know right away if you're enclosing information they requested.
- Tie in your customer's request to some additional selling points. Include some features and how they will benefit the customer in a helpful and friendly manner.
- Offer an invitation to one location.
- Use a friendly closing.

BONUS LETTER

It's easy to see why Mary Kay Cosmetics, Inc. has such a large and loyal customer base when you read the following letter to a Mary Kay customer.

This response to a product sample inquiry is used not only to sell the customer on the product requested but also to remind the customer about the benefits of other services.

Mary Kay Cosmetics, Inc. makes it easy for the customer to respond by providing a representative's name and phone number locally, as well as a toll-free number to Customer Services Headquarters.

MARY KAY

December 19, 1990

Dear {new customer}:

Thank you for your recent inquiry requesting a sample of Mary Kay Nighttime Recovery System. This revolutionary new product is a combination of gel and cream that helps minimize the visible signs of damage from environmental impurities and weather extremes. Also enclosed is a copy of our most recent beauty book, which provides skin care instructions and product information.

An Independent Mary Kay Beauty Consultant is specially trained to help you with all your skin care and glamour needs. During a personalized consultation, she will determine your specific skin type, discuss the proper skin care formulas to use, and show you the best glamour shades for your coloring. Plus you will have the opportunity to sample products and apply them yourself during your complimentary facial.

To arrange a complimentary facial, we have a Beauty Consultant in your area who would be happy to assist you. Her name is {bcname}, and you can reach her at {phone}.

If for any reason you cannot reach {customer representative{, or you should have any other questions, please call our Customer Service Department toll-free at 1-800-MARY KAY.

Thank you for your interest in Mary Kay Cosmetics.

Sincerely,

{Name}
Senior Vice President Marketing Group

Enclosures

cc: {representative}

3.5 Answering a Request for Merchandise That Is No Longer Available

Situation The robe Joan Elliot ordered from last season's R.R. Dean catalog is no longer available. The seller needs to notify the customer that her order cannot be filled. Ideally, the seller should offer other choices that might satisfy the customer's request. If none is available, the objective is to keep the customer despite losing this one sale. There should be an emphasis on service and relationship.

The Letter Dear Ms. Elliot:

Your request for shipment of a Polar Plush robe, White, size Large, has been passed along to me. It was one of our most popular items and I'm sorry to tell you that stock sold out very quickly. Since it was a Buyer's Special—and a seasonal item, too—we are not able to back-order for you as is our usual procedure.

In checking our winter robe supply, however, I have found two other styles that might suit your needs and your budget. Catalog photos of each are enclosed. I've also put an inventory hold on one of each in the event that you choose to place an order.

While you're certainly under no obligation, I'd appreciate your letting me know your decision. At R.R. Dean, meeting our customer's needs is most important to us. If the enclosed choices are not right for you, I'd be happy to see if there's some other way we can fill your order.

Again, please feel free to call me at the phone number above, or write if you prefer. You are very important to us, and I'd welcome the opportunity to personally assist you.

Sincerely,

Customer Service Representative

Key Points

- Explain right away that you will not be able to fill the order and why.
- Offer other choices to show your company's capabilities and that you're willing to give customers personalized attention.
- Ask customers to respond. Let them know you care about serving them.
- Repeat your willingness to personally assist them.

3.6 Answering a Request to Deal with Staff Who Are No Longer with the Company

Situation Confidence and familiarity play a part in ensuring that your customers keep coming back to *you*, rather than going to your competitors. So, when a member of your staff leaves, it is very important that you smooth over any staff change or transitional period with their customers. The Vice President of Sales at BSS is writing to John Conway of Conway Systems to let him know that his account rep has left, and to introduce her replacement. Emphasis is on the *continued* high-quality service the customer will receive.

The Letter Dear Mr. Conway:

Your letter to Marcia Briggs arrived on my desk just as I was writing to tell you that she is no longer with Business Service Specialties.

I'm sure you'll agree that Marcia was one of our most valuable and respected service reps. And I know you'll be as sorry as we were that personal family matters required her to unexpectedly move out of state and leave BSS.

While this means a new agent has been assigned to your account, I believe you'll be extremely pleased with the level of service and expertise Sandra Bergner will be able to give you. As an eight-year veteran with our main headquarters, Sandra is well versed in our entire product line and has the technical expertise to back it up.

To ensure a smooth transition for your account, Marcia left extensive notes regarding all your special preferences and needs. Sandra will be calling you within the week to introduce herself and set up an appointment to review this information.

All of us at Business Service Specialties are dedicated to giving you the highest level of service possible—the same level that has kept Conway Systems our customer since 1986. I'd be happy to hear from you if there's any way at all I can assist you during this transition.

Sincerely,

V.P. Sales

Key Points

- Tell the customer that there has been a staff change.
- Offer a positive explanation why. Let the customer know who will now be handling the account.
- Show that you have made a special effort to make this transition a smooth one. State what will happen next.
- Remind the customer that you have a long and successful relationship. Extend your personal willingness to help.

BONUS LETTER

When the authors of this book asked the prestigious Tiffany & Co. to share one of their customer service letters with us for this book, they said no.

It was not surprising, though, that a company known worldwide for quality, elegance, and customer care would be able to turn us down with such eloquence and grace.

Tiffany & Co. was nice enough to let us share their letter to us with you.

TIFFANY & CO.
FIFTH AVENUE & 57TH STREET
NEW YORK 10022
212-755-8000

June 4, 1991

Mr. Edward W. Werz
Author
Information Publishing, Inc.
79 Carley Avenue
Huntington, NY 11743

Dear Mr. Werz,

Thank you for the invitation to provide samples of our customer service letters for your upcoming book THE COMPLETE CUSTOMER SERVICE LETTER. On behalf of Tiffany & Co. may I say how terribly pleased I am to learn of your recognition of our company's customer service communications.

It is a great privilege to consider your request that examples of our customer service letters be made available for publication in your upcoming book. Due to the nature of our business, however, we would prefer that these letters not be considered or provided for publishing purposes.

I expect your upcoming book will be a valuable tool for many companies as Customer Service seems to be the most talked about area of business today. Best wishes to you for a most successful publication.

Sincerely,

Marion Davidson
Director
Public Relations

3.7 Answering a Request for a Product Not Available Through the Company

Situation DecoFrame manufactures a wide variety of decorative photo albums. In fact, they believe they carry the largest assortment in the field. Nevertheless, one of their customers has ordered a model that is not part of their product line. The account representative needs to tell this to the customer in a way that maintains their good relationship. He also wants to try to keep the sale if at all possible.

The Letter Dear Mr. Snodgrass:

We were extremely pleased to receive your request for our mock alligator photo albums in a 4×4-inch size.

As the leading manufacturer of decorative photograph albums, DecoFrame offers over 200 sizes and styles to choose from. Imagine our frustration, then, to receive your order for a style and size combination not included in the DecoFrame product line.

We value your business and have always been able to supply Gabriella Gift Shops with the merchandise you've needed when you've needed it. We'd like to be able to maintain this record!

One option would be to substitute our Style C432, a pressed leather case available in six colors. I've enclosed catalog style sheets and several samples for you to present to your purchasing committee. These are not offered in any other locations in Wasau County and might meet your needs if you're looking for a piece that's up to Gabriella's usual high quality and reasonable pricing, as well as a unique model we can offer you exclusively.

A second choice would be for us to produce a custom product to meet your specifications. If this is of interest, DecoFrame would need additional information on delivery dates and expected purchases over the next six months.

We look forward to working with you to find the best solution possible. I'll telephone later this week after you've had a chance to review the options—or call me sooner if that's more convenient.

Sincerely,

Sales Manager

Key Points

- Acknowledge the order and thank your customer.
- Inform the customer that the product ordered is not available through your company but remind them of the wide range of products you do carry.
- Tell your customers how important they are to you and how well you've served them in the past.
- Offer other ways *your company* might still fill customers' needs. Show that you're trying to work with them.
- Establish a next contact to resolve the order in a way favorable to your company. Even if you ultimately lose the order, you want them to know you've done everything possible.

3.8 Answering a Request for Visit by a Sales Representative

Situation Canfield's, an office equipment and supplies catalog company, has asked to see a sales rep from Sunspot printers. Sunspot has done some small printing jobs for Canfield in the past but has not been able to get a larger percentage of their business. All contact so far has been over the phone and through the mail. Now, Canfield is considering Sunspot to print a major catalog and wants to see a sales representative. In his letter, the Sunspot rep wants to show his company's interest in servicing the account and in seting up an appointment as quickly as possible.

The Letter Dear Mr. Fabrian:

In response to your letter of August 25, I'd like to introduce myself as the Sunspot representative who will be working with your account.

We were extremely pleased to hear that you're considering Sunspot as exclusive printers for Canfield's print work. It was especially gratifying to hear that we had been recommended to you by several associates. While we've worked with Canfield's on a limited basis in the past, our relationship was confined to the phone and mail. We strongly agree that an in-person meeting is required to discuss the type of program you have in mind.

I can be in the Long Island area the week of September 10 and hope to meet then to review your needs and how Sunspot can best serve you. Please tell me what day and time will be most convenient... or if a different week is preferable.

The printing business is extremely competitive. But after we've met, I believe you'll understand why Sunspot has such a fine reputation and customers who work with us year after year.

I will call you on September 4 if I have not heard from you by then. I'm looking forward to working with you and the Canfield staff.

Sincerely,

Account Executive

Key Points

- Introduce yourself and let the customer know you're responding to the inquiry.
- Express your pleasure at the possibility of doing business with them. Mention your previous connection to them—a job well done, a recommendation.
- State when you're available to see them and remember to be flexible.
- Mention some of the positive qualities your company is known for.
- Tell the customer when you will call. Close with your positive expectations of future business.

4

Letters Explaining Company Policy

Before you can begin to write letters explaining your company's policies, your company must *have* specific policies in place to explain. So first let us stress the value and importance of determining how your company should best handle the variety of situations that commonly occur in your type of business.

The specifics of your company's policy on any issue will be determined by factors that include the type of business you run, the type of customer you serve, how your competitors handle these issues, legal considerations, and more. Company policy allows you to handle your valuable customers with fairness and consistency. It allows you to respond promptly when a question is raised; you don't have to take time to consider how best to address the situation. Fair, well thought-out company policies reinforce your image as a company with sound business sense, a company that knows what it's doing.

Information on company policy should be readily available to customers. For instance, policy can be printed directly on sales slips, contracts, or order forms. Yet, even when it is, customers often do not read the fine print or pay attention to it at the time of purchase. It is often the seller's job to notify the customer of the content of relevant company policy and of the reason for it.

Just like any other rules, company policies can be changed or adapted to specific situations. While it is always best to have a policy to handle the majority of situations, any customer-sensitive company must be able to show flexibility if the situation warrants it.

Key Points

- Company policies should be determined and in place for all the common customer service situations that can be expected in your type of business.
- Establishing a company policy allows you to show consistency and fairness in the treatment of customers.
- Company policy allows you to handle customer service inquiries promptly.
- A sound set of company policies project a positive company image.
- While customers, of course, prefer policies that meet their needs, it is often easier to accept a "no" if it is presented as an established, in-force policy. Legally, too, companies are at risk if they enforce certain rules for some customers but not for others.
- Despite the need for consistency, companies need to show flexibility on policies if the situation warrants it.

4.1 Explaining Price Policy

Situation Because of escalating prices from suppliers, a manufacturer must pass a price increase on to its customers. A letter is sent announcing this new policy.

The Letter Dear ______:

Writing to good customers to inform them about a price increase is never an easy task. Fortunately, along with the bad news comes some good news.

Over the last six months, the price of petroleum-based products has increased. As you know, our plastic file holders are produced almost exclusively with polypropylene, an oil-based thermoplastic resin. Our costs have increased by 8 percent.

We have held our prices as long as possible, absorbing this price increase without raising prices. Unfortunately, it is no longer possible to maintain our old price levels.

Now for the good news. To lessen the impact of the price increase, we have invested in new equipment that will recycle waste material. The savings from this process will offset the higher cost of material by almost 50 percent. Therefore, our new price list (enclosed) reflects only a 4-percent increase.

While no one likes higher prices, we are confident that our new price structure is among the lowest in the industry. These prices are in effect as of June 1. Any orders received before that date will be honored at the old prices.

Thank you for your past business. We look forward to serving you in the future.

Sincerely,

President

Key Points

- Inform the customer of the price increase in a personal manner. State why prices must increase.
- When feasible, offer some good news as well.
- Offer the customer an opportunity to order at the old price level and spell out the date when the higher prices go into effect.
- If the competition's prices have also increased, or are higher, subtly make reference to that fact.
- Close by thanking customers for their past patronage.

4.2 Explaining Delivery Policy

Situation When a new customer purchases from AmTech, a wholesale supplier of building products, a letter is sent explaining their delivery policy. Because the charges for the delivery of building materials can be a significant part of the cost of supplies, it is important to fully explain the company's policy when a new customer comes on board.

The Letter Dear ______:

Welcome to AmTech.

We'd like to explain AmTech's delivery policy so that you can take full advantage of our fast and economical shipping program.

Most of AmTech's 16,000+ products are in stock and on the shelf for immediate shipment. Generally, you can expect delivery within 5 to 8 working days ARO. If a product should be out of stock due to unusual demand, we notify you either by phone or mail within 24 hours of receipt of your order. At that time, we provide you with a firm delivery date.

We ship by common carrier or UPS, depending on the size of your order. All shipments are routed the most economical way unless you require special or overnight handling. All shipments have a complete packing slip attached to the outside of the carton.

You can also benefit from our policy of absorbing all shipping and handling costs for prepaid orders over $250.

This saving can significantly reduce your costs on large orders.

If you purchase on open account, our terms are FOB warehouse, San Mateo, California.

Should you have any questions about our delivery policy, please do not hesitate to call me.

Sincerely,

Sales Manager

P.S.: At Amtech, we constantly strive to have the most efficient, customer-friendly delivery system in the business. Our 35,000 satisfied customers depend on it. You can too!

Key Points

- Explain why you are writing. Use this opportunity to make a positive statement about your service.
- Describe your policy in a clear and concise manner that supports your image of organization and efficiency.
- If one aspect of your service is outstanding or offers exceptional value to your customer, now is a good time to present it.
- Reassure the customer that you will personally answer any questions.
- Add a P.S. reinforcing your commitment to delivery excellence.

4.3 Explaining Return Policy

Situation A customer has sent a letter to Spectacular Publishing indicating that he/she wishes to return a recent order. The company responds by sending a letter explaining its policy on returns.

The Letter

Dear ______:

I have received your request for clarification of our return policy. I am sorry if the product that you ordered did not meet your expectations. Our no-risk return policy should make resolving your problem easy.

All of Spectacular Publishing's products are sold on a 30-day free trial. If you are not satisfied with a product for any reason, it may be returned for a complete refund or credit within 30 days of receipt. A sale is therefore not final until you are completely satisfied.

If you would like to return a product, the procedure is simple. Just call our toll-free customer service line and ask for a return authorization number. Include that number in your shipment back to us. We will immediately credit your account and send you a refund check. Or, if you like, you can use your credit against a new purchase now or in the future. Just send us instructions on how you would like this handled.

Again, I am sorry that you were not pleased with your order. I'm sure your next purchase from Spectacular Publishing will meet with your approval.

Sincerely,

Customer Service Manager

Key Points

- Explain why you are writing. Express your regrets that the customer was not pleased with the purchase.
- Explain your policy in simple, easy-to-follow terms.
- Apologize again for the customer's dissatisfaction.
- Express your expectation that the customer will buy again from your company and that future purchases will be satisfactory.

4.4 Explaining Product Sampling Policy

Situation A school district has written requesting sample copies of publications for possible use in its program. The publisher responds to the request quickly with a letter and sample package.

The Letter Dear ______:

Thank you for your interest in our product line. In your letter, you described your organization's efforts in working with at-risk youth to prevent delinquent behavior and substance abuse. We applaud the important contribution you are making to your community.

You requested sample copies of six of our titles for possible use in your program. We are pleased to send these to you, along with two other titles that we think you will also want to see. In addition, we've included our new catalog describing all our publications.

You'll notice that special quantity prices are listed on page 23 of the catalog. The more booklets you order, the more you save. Plus, you can combine titles to reach the highest quantity discount and qualify for the highest savings.

To order, simply return the order form to us by mail or fax—or call us on our toll-free telephone number 800-555-1234.

Again, thank you for your interest in our publications and for the important service that you provide.

Sincerely,

Customer Service Manager

Key Points

- Thank the customer for the inquiry.
- Personalize your response with references to the customer's special interests.
- Describe exactly how you will fulfill the request for samples.
- If possible, offer an additional sample.
- Tell the customer what step to take next; how to order, where to call, and so on.
- Close by thanking the customer again.

4.5 Explaining Service Calls Policy

Situation TriState Garden Supplies has been contacted by a customer with a broken lawn mower. Since the customer is no longer entitled to repairs under the product warrantee, the Service Manager must notify the customer of the company's repair policy.

The Letter Dear ______:

We're sorry to hear that your Turbo 1000 Lawn Clipper is in need of repair. As you know, your mower was purchased on May 20, seven months ago.

When you purchased the machine, a six-month service agreement, with no charge for parts or labor, was included. Now that you are past the expiration date, service work will require a charge according to the enclosed schedule.

TriState Garden Supplies is the largest distributor of garden tools and equipment in this area, servicing more lawn movers than any of our competitors. Because of our extensive experience and expertise, all repairs are guaranteed for 120 days—an offer that you won't find anyplace else.

You can be confident that TriState will repair your equipment exclusively with factory-authorized parts. To arrange an appointment for your repair, or to have our convenient pickup service visit you, call 800-555-3200.

Sincerely

Service Manager

Key Points

- Acknowledge the customer's request for repair.
- Explain the status of the customer's service agreement.
- If the customer is to be charged, describe the benefits of using your company's repair department.
- When possible, point out any of your special or exclusive services.
- Close with a positive statement about your service capabilities. Make the repair process sound as routine as possible.

4.6 Explaining Credit Policy

Situation After a small first order, Regal Department Stores has placed a very large order for office equipment. Amos Office must establish credit for the new customer before the order can be shipped. A letter explaining Amos's policy is immediately sent.

The Letter Dear ______:

Thank you for your purchase order #23456 for 48 Fireproof Lateral Files. These products are in stock and will be available for shipment in 5 days.

In order to ship the order on open account, we must first establish credit terms for you. I've enclosed a credit application and a commercial reference form. Please complete these and return them using our Federal Express account #0000-0000-0 or by fax. As soon as we receive the information, we will process your request. Normally, we can provide credit within 48 hours.

We are very pleased that you have chosen Amos Office as your supplier. You can count on us for exceptional value, quality products, and quick, reliable service.

If you have any questions regarding the credit application or our policies, please call me. I look forward to working with you in the future.

Sincerely,

Amos Cross
President

Key Points

- Acknowledge the new order and thank the customer for it.
- Explain your policy for establishing credit.
- Tell the customer exactly what must be done. Where possible, make it easy for the customer to comply.
- Suggest that the customer call with any unanswered questions or concerns.

4.7 Explaining Holiday Credit Policy

Situation Heathcrest Department Store wants to inform its customers of a liberal credit policy for holiday shoppers. A letter is sent to all customers before Thanksgiving, explaining the credit terms and encouraging shoppers to buy early and at Heathcrest!

The Letter Dear Customer:

There's excitement in the air here at Heathcrest! We're busily filling our shelves with beautiful, new, and surprisingly affordable gift items to make your holiday shopping easy and enjoyable.

Best of all, to ensure that you can better plan your budget for this expensive time of the year, we're introducing a special Heathcrest Holiday Credit Plan just for you.

It's really simple. When you come to any Heathcrest store, just show the enclosed card to your salesperson prior to making your purchase. You'll be able to charge merchandise up to your account limit and not pay until February of next year. And it's interest free!

So why not come visit your closest Heathcrest store today? See the festive holiday decorations and shop to your heart's content.

Sincerely,

Store Manager

P.S.: If you still have any questions, call our Holiday Shoppers Line at 800-555-3000.

P.P.S.: To speak to our convenient Holiday Shopping Service—they'll do it all for you—call 800-555-3200.

Key Points

- Begin with an expression of holiday spirit.
- Describe the specifics of your holiday credit policy. Make it as simple and as inviting as you can.
- Emphasize any unusual aspects of your program, such as no interest charged on holiday purchases.
- Encourage customers to visit your store early and to take advantage of a program designed especially for them.

4.8 Explaining Policy Regarding Product Demonstrations

Situation A corporate customer is considering upgrading the software it uses for inventory management. Since several staff members would be involved in the final decision, a request has been made for an on-premises demonstration of the system under consideration. A letter is sent to the questioner outlining the product demonstration options.

The Letter Dear _______:

Thank you for your interest in upgrading your Recordkeeper 4.0 software to the newest release, 6.0. We are very pleased to hear that the system you purchased from us two years ago has proven itself to you. Your desire to improve your current system can be a very sound decision for the growth of your firm.

We understand that you are interested in having Recordkeeper 6.0 demonstrated to your staff. We agree that this is the ideal way to see the product's capabilities and advanced features firsthand. Compuworks, Inc. offers two convenient demonstration options.

First, we conduct classes on Recordkeeper 6.0 in our training center twice each month. You can schedule your staff to participate in a two-session evening course. Obviously, the benefit of this option is that you do not lose any time in the office. All attendees also receive in-depth, hands-on training. There's no charge for this training in our facility.

Second, we can also schedule a product demonstration in your office at a time convenient to you and your staff. Here, the advantage is that you can actually see the product work in your business environment with the demonstration focus on your company's specific needs. While there is a charge for this service, it will be deducted from the final price if you choose to install a Recordkeeper 6.0 system.

We'll be happy to work with you in whatever way you decide is best. I'm sure you'll want to discuss the options, and I've enclosed a price sheet covering the demonstration possibilities at your location. I'll follow up with you next week. Don't hesitate to call if you have any additional questions before then.

Sincerely,

President

Key Points

- Thank your customer for requesting a product demonstration.
- Point out the good business sense that would be shown by purchasing the system or product to be demonstrated.
- Discuss the demonstration options available to the questioner.
- Let the customer know that you'll be happy with whichever option is chosen.
- State when you will next contact the customer for a decision.

4.9 Explaining Policy on Warranties/Guarantees

Situation After a purchase of its fitness equipment, the Exer-Ride Company sends each new customer a letter explaining its generous product warranty. This sale follow-up helps build goodwill and customer loyalty.

The Letter Dear ______:

Thank you for your purchase of an Exer-Ride Bicycle. We are sure you will thoroughly enjoy using this remarkable piece of fitness equipment.

As you know, your Exer-Ride comes with a full year warranty. We will repair and replace any defective part at no cost to you during this period, including the cost of shipping your Exer-Ride to our maintenance center and back to you. This warranty is effective for any problem due to normal use.

If you do encounter a problem, please consult the owner's manual for our toll-free help line. Often, one of our customer service counselors can suggest a simple adjustment to help you fix the problem. If not, they will arrange for a pickup of your bicycle for repair.

Most Exer-Ride owners never encounter a performance problem. But it's good to know that, if you should, you're fully covered. That's the Exer-Ride warranty!

Again, thanks for your purchase.

Sincerely,

Judy Quill

Key Points

- Thank the customer for the purchase.
- Explain the warranty/guarantee. Point out all the features that will benefit the customer.
- Describe any other services that are available.
- Close by offering thanks again.

4.10 Explaining Gratuity Policy

Situation Maddy's department store prides itself on personal service to its customers. Often, during the holiday season, satisfied customers offer their favorite clerk a holiday gift. Maddy's wishes to discourage gratuities and is thus sending a letter notifying customers of their policy.

The Letter Dear ______:

The holiday season is upon us! And all of us at Maddy's want to thank you—our valued customer—for your business this year.

We'd also like to take this opportunity to state our policy regarding gratuities during the holiday season. Maddy's does not permit its employees to accept gratuities of any kind. Our employees are well compensated for the work they do on behalf of Maddy's and our customers.

Maddy employees' extraordinary attention to detail, along with their friendly, positive attitude and desire to be of genuine assistance, is expected as normal service. Your satisfaction and continued patronage are thanks enough.

So please, no gratuities. Naturally, your thanks and season's greetings are encouraged.

Again, from the entire staff, happy holiday and a healthy new year!

Sincerely,

Store Manager

Key Points

- Begin in a personal, friendly manner. Remember, you are communicating with established customers and are asking a favor of them.
- Explain your policy. Use the opportunity to reinforce your company's excellent customer service record.
- Close with a warm expression of thanks.

4.11 Explaining Shipping Policy

Situation A new customer has placed an initial order with Axco Distributors. Since shipping costs can significantly affect the price of the order, the customer wishes to receive an explanation of the company's shipping policy. A letter is sent to the customer with details.

The Letter

Dear ______:

Thank you for your first order. We are pleased to welcome you as a new customer.

Your sales representative, Ellen Struthers, mentioned that you would like us to explain our shipping policy.

Our shipping terms are FOB our Danbury, Connecticut factory. This means that the customer pays for the shipping from the factory to his/her location. Shipping is arranged the least expensive way by common carrier unless other instructions are given.

Of special interest is our policy to pay all shipping charges for prepaid orders. Often, the savings on shipping for prepaid orders can be significant. In fact, over 50 percent of our customers order on a prepayment basis to save the shipping costs.

Naturally, we can arrange rush shipping and special packaging to meet your requirements.

I hope your questions have been answered. Please call me if I can be of further assistance.

Sincerely,

Stan Jasper
Traffic Manager

Key Points

- Express thanks for the order or inquiry.
- Describe the purpose of the letter.
- Offer an explanation of the policy in easy-to-follow language.
- When your policy is of benefit to the customer, point it out.
- Encourage customers to call if they have further questions.

4.12 Explaining Return Policy on Custom-Manufactured Products

Situation Design Gift Items, Inc. has received a request to return an order of custom-imprinted coffee mugs. The customer has decided to close the store for which the imprinted mugs were ordered and wishes to return the items. DGI's existing return policy is detailed in a written response.

The Letter Dear ______:

We have received your letter of April 5 requesting permission to return your order #B345 and for a credit to be applied to your account.

Upon reviewing your order file, we find that this particular order was for 250 custom-imprinted mugs. Our policy on returns of customized products is clearly stated on page 24 of our catalog and again on the order form that you filled out.

Unfortunately, we cannot accept any return on merchandise that has been specifically imprinted at a customer's request.

We are sure you can understand our position since your order cannot be put back into inventory. As you know, all other products in our catalog (without imprint) are sold on a 30-day returnable basis. We sincerely wish we could offer that special return policy to you. In this case, however, we cannot.

Enclosed is a copy of the signed proof for your custom order that you approved prior to imprinting. We're sorry about your change of plans and our inability to grant your request.

We would appreciate your payment of the enclosed invoice at your earliest convenience. We value your business and hope to be able to serve you in the future.

Sincerely,

Customer Service Manager

Key Points

- Acknowledge the customer request for a return and credit.
- Review the specifics of the order and then state your company's policy covering this type of situation.
- Sympathize with the customer's dilemma, but be firm about your inability to accept the return.
- Express your expectation that business with this customer will continue.

4.13 Explaining Policy on Return of Sale Item

Situation Star Photographic Supplies has received a customer request to return a camera and accessory items purchased during Star's annual presummer sale. The store's General Manager sends a letter explaining Star's policy on the return of sale items.

The Letter Dear Mr. Roberts:

Bob Allen asked me to contact you regarding your request to return the Minolta MX200 and accessories you purchased at our recent Spring Sale Bonanza. I'm sorry to hear that you had to cancel your summer tour of the Greek Islands. Hopefully, you'll be able to reschedule it soon.

While Star's Returns Policy is printed on the back of all sales slips, I'm happy to review the part relevant to your purchase. You may also want to refer to Item #4 of that document.

We try to make our Annual Spring Sale Bonanza a truly spectacular sales event. To offer you the best prices possible, we cannot provide customers with the same liberal return policy available on items purchased at full price. Our Return Policy allows for exchanges only, up to 14 days from purchase. After this two-week grace period, all purchases of sale items are final. Therefore, we must decline your request.

Your Minolta MX200 is an exceptional piece of equipment, and the price you paid is not available anywhere else. Despite your change of plans, I'm sure you'll find many other opportunities to enjoy it. Please let me know if I can be of any further assistance.

Sincerely,

General Manager

Key Points

- Tell the customer why you are writing. If appropriate, let the customer know that you are aware of his or her personal situation.
- If your policy is included on paperwork already in the customer's hands, make the customer aware of this.
- Restate the policy in a simple, clear, and firm way.
- If your policy is not to accept sale returns, include a statement about the high quality or value of the purchase. Reaffirm the customer's good choice to have made the purchase.
- Offer additional assistance, if needed. End on a positive note, even if you have been unable to meet the customer's demands.

4.14 Explaining Discontinuance of Company Service

Situation Lynn Mellon's Marketing Services company has discontinued her two-hour copy consultation. While this was an extremely popular service, it did not prove itself to be cost effective or effective in drawing customers in for more substantial programs. Ms. Mellon has written the following letter to send customers inquiring about this service.

The Letter Dear ______:

Thank you so much for your interest in the Lynn Mellon's Marketing Services and the Mini-Mail Consultation. Regretfully, we no longer offer this service.

I reviewed the information you sent regarding your company and its marketing needs, and I do provide both a product and service that might work well for you.

A four-hour audio program, entitled "Copy That Sells," includes four tapes and a 25-page workbook. It covers how to create a basic marketing strategy and write effective advertising. I've enclosed a descriptive brochure and several reviews that will tell you more about the specific skills and techniques covered. The price for this program is $79.95.

A four-session workshop is scheduled for your area this summer. This will be sponsored by Broadhurst Community Center for local service businesses like yours. While it will not offer quite the same personal attention as the Mini-Mall Consultation you had requested, the number of participants will be limited. That means each of you will be able to ask all the questions you desire and complete one sales letter, flyer, or other advertising piece to your satisfaction. The price for this will be $129.00.

I'd be happy to discuss these and other options with you in more detail and will phone you next week. I'm sure we can find a satisfactory solution.

Sincerely,

Lynn Mellon
President

Key Points

- Thank customers for their interest in your company and the service requested.
- Tell customers that this service is no longer available. If there is a reason for the discontinuance that is simple and does not entail proprietary information, let the customer know what it is.
- Show customers that you've given thought to their needs. If at all possible, offer available options that might still meet their needs.
- Express your desire to work with customers to satisfy their needs.

4.15 Explaining Out-of-Stock/Back Order Situations

Situation Crawford and Hayes Carpet Mills has received an order from Carpet World for 7000 yards of Ultra Plush Jade Green pile carpeting. Since C&H has no existing stock for that style and color, a letter must be sent to notify the customer of the out-of-stock situation and C&H's policy regarding back orders.

The Letter Dear Mr. Raleigh:

We were pleased to receive your August 8 order #G4362 for 12 line items from our most recent Ultra Plush catalog. The items listed on the attached confirmation are in stock and will be delivered to you the week of August 20, as requested.

Product #72, Ultra Plush Jade, however, is temporarily out of stock. This item is being put on back order.

Our back-order policy is as follows: As we are constantly replenishing our stock, we expect that no item will be out of stock longer than four weeks. If delivery in four weeks or sooner does not suit your needs, we will cancel this back order. Please call our customer service number with instructions regarding this back-ordered item as soon as possible. If we do not hear from you by Tuesday, August 20, this back order will be cancelled.

At Crawford & Hayes, we do our best to maintain ample inventory to fulfill our customers' requirements. Occasionally, an item will sell out because of unusually high demand. We apologize for any inconvenience this may have caused you.

Mr. Raleigh, thank you for your business. If you have any questions, please call Bob Smith, your Customer Service Representative.

Sincerely,

Sales Manager

Key Points

- Acknowledge the customer's order and the order status.
- Define your company's back order policy as simply as possible. Make sure to clearly state your order cancellation policy as well.
- Include a company policy statement regarding adequate stock maintenance and your general concern for customer satisfaction.
- Thank the customer for their business.

5

New Customer Letters

New customers represent a very special segment of your customer list and need to be treated that way. Often considerable effort and expense go into acquiring new customers. Once the new clients are yours, you must ask whether you are doing everything you can to make sure they stay yours. Studies have shown that it takes three purchases by customers to create a new buying habit. So that first order should not be enough to make you sit back and relax.

One way to cement this important relationship is to make sure that all customer contacts are faultless in their presentation. The appropriate tone, a professional presentation with no typos or grammatical errors, and accurate information should always be the clear qualities of your correspondence.

For new customers especially, you want to build trust and rapport. You want to show that you are knowledgeable about and interested in your customers' businesses and needs. You want to demonstrate that you care about them, and that you are willing to go the extra step to ensure their satisfaction. Some companies do this by offering a welcome kit or package with information about themselves and all their products and services, samples if possible, a special price or discount, or even a new customer gift. You especially want to assure customers that they will not be taken for granted as soon as they place an order.

You may want to make a unique or special offer to show that they have made a good decision in going with your company, or extend yourself with a more personal invitation to get to know new customers better. Whatever your approach, remember that you want your letters to new customers to reinforce the importance of their status and build on the relationship that you have started.

Key Points

- You've spent time and money to get new customers, and now you must make sure that all your customer contacts will reinforce their decision to buy from you and your company.
- All letters going out from your company should be flawless in tone and presentation.
- Construct letters that build trust and rapport between you and your new customers.
- Let your new customer letter reinforce the image you want to project and the type of relationship you want to develop.
- When possible, offer a special "getting to know you" gift or offer.

5.1 Welcome to the Area Letter

Situation Faxmobile, a fax equipment and supplies sales, service, and leasing company, is about to sign a contract with an import/export firm new to the area. When Herb Barnes, Faxmobile's president, hears of this from one of his sales reps, he writes the customer (Mr. Bernstein) a welcome letter. This is designed to position Faxmobile as a new friend, someone on whom Mr. Bernstein can rely while his firm gets settled into their new facility. If Faxmobile can establish a good customer relationship now, he will certainly have created some strong customer loyalty.

The Letter Dear Mr. Bernstein:

As President of Faxmobile, it gives me great pleasure to welcome you to the Brent Forest area.

Joel Leewood, our sales representative handling your account has told me about your company and we're looking forward not only to supplying and servicing your 25 Model R34 machines, but also to assisting you in any way possible as you get settled in your new facility.

I understand that, in your business, the ability to transmit information cross-country and cross-continent is key. And Faxmobile wants to be the type of supplier you can count on to make that easier for you. Let us worry about keeping your machines in working order so that you can keep your eye on business.

Joel has prepared a supply/service contract that should meet all the criteria you outlined for him. And for our best customers, there's even a quantity discount program for supplies that you may want to take advantage of.

When Joel meets with you next Tuesday to review your contract, he'll also bring a booklet about the area that you and your employees might find interesting. I know that it takes a while to find your way around someplace new, both business-wise and personally. We hope you'll let us contribute to making your adjustment period a brief one.

I look forward to meeting you in the near future. Perhaps once you're settled in, you, Joel, and I can meet for lunch.

Sincerely,

Herbert Barnes
President

P.S.: I understand from Joel that you're an avid golfer. There are some spectacular courses within an hour's drive from here. Let me know if you're interested.

Key Points

- Open with a friendly welcoming statement.
- Express pleasure at serving the account.
- Show an understanding of your customer's needs and how your company will be able to work with them.
- Let them know what will happen next. Make a special offer.
- Add a personal comment and offer any assistance needed to make the newcomers feel they can call on you.
- Use a friendly close with a personal invitation, if appropriate.

5.2 Welcome to Your New Job

Situation Sarah Newbridge is the Classified Advertising Manager for a trade paper, *Customer Service News*. A steady, though fairly new customer, Mansford and Sons, has just replaced Bob Hotchkins, her contact there, with someone new. In her letter, Sarah wants to welcome the new Personnel Manager, introduce herself, and present her services in a way that will help assure buying continuity.

The Letter Dear Louise:

I just heard the news that you have taken over the position of Personnel Manager at Mansford & Sons and want to welcome you. I'm sure you already know that Mansford is an excellent company; you'll also soon find out that you're working with one of the nicest and most competent staffs around.

I don't know if you had much chance to review things with Bob Hotchkins since his schedule necessitated his leaving so quickly. Bob has been successfully using the *Customer Service News* Classified Section to locate and hire the best in Customer Service staff for both your main fulfillment location and the two smaller telemarketing groups. We certainly hope to continue this success under your direction.

While I know it takes a while to familiarize yourself with new surroundings and responsibilities, I hope we'll soon be able to meet—to get acquainted and review Mansford's upcoming staffing needs.

If there's any way we can assist you in the meantime, please call. I will phone you in two weeks to set up an appointment. Maybe we can even include lunch, if you have the time. I'm looking forward to speaking to you then.

Sincerely,

Sarah Newbridge
Classified Advertising Manager

Key Points

- Even though the two haven't met, Sarah can address Louise in a friendly and somewhat informal manner. It introduces Sarah in terms of her existing relationship with Mansford & Sons.
- Sarah wants to show Louise that she is already a trusted supplier. She presents herself confidently in expectation of the continuation of this relationship.
- Sarah acknowledges Louise's "new" status and that she's available to work with her.
- Again, a warm and friendly close is appropriate here, to make the newcomer feel more at ease.

5.3 Cover Letter to Accompany a Catalog/Brochure

Situation A customer has purchased a new word processor from a local retailer. When the customer returns his warranty to Jonesboro, the manufacturer, a letter, and catalog offering accessory products and supplies is sent.

The Letter Dear Mr. Warren:

Recently you purchased a X2000 Jonesboro Word Processor. By now, you've probably had a chance to use the system and appreciate its state-of-the-art features.

To make ordering supplies easier for our customers, Jonesboro offers a direct-from-the-manufacturer hotline. We've enclosed our discount catalog and price list with a postage-paid order card. If you prefer to call in your order, our toll-free number—1-800-555-7777—is open 7 days a week, 24 hours a day.

You'll notice that we've packaged ribbon cartridges in boxes of 24. By purchasing in bulk, you save over 40 percent off the single cartridge price. While this may not suit every customer's needs, it's the lowest price available anywhere if you can take advantage of it.

Thank you for your order and supply business. We hope you'll find our direct-from-the-manufacturer hotline an economical and convenient way to order supplies.

Sincerely,

Special Services Manager

Key Points

- Remind the customer of the initial purchase. Express confidence in his or her satisfaction with the product.
- Introduce the catalog/brochure or materials that you've enclosed. Focus on how the customer will benefit from these services, such as savings, convenience, guarantees, delivery, etc.
- Point out one item, discount, or service that offers exceptional value.
- Express thanks for the customer's business while reinforcing the benefits of doing business with your company.

5.4 Letter Requesting a Referral

Situation As the saying goes, "Timing is everything." When requesting a customer referral, that is especially true. While you would hope that your relationships with long-time customers are strong enough to ask them for referrals, proceed with caution when approaching new customers. In the next letter, Bob Stone, a Cramer consultant, waits until after the successful completion of their first big project to ask the head of Ryan Technologies for a referral.

The Letter Dear Mr. Ryan:

Even though compliments are not often given in the business world, I have one for your firm. If Cramer Computer Consultants were asked to describe their ideal client, the description would fit Ryan Technologies perfectly. The quality of your products, your excellent staff, the consideration and respect you show for both customers and suppliers all contribute to your success and your value as a client.

Similarly, based on Cramer's completion of the RAM2 Project on deadline and under budget, I feel confident that you are more than satisfied with Cramer's competence, level of service, and cost-effectiveness.

At this point, I'm sure you're asking yourself why I'm telling you this. And I confess that, even though what I say is true, there is a reason.

The reason is that all of us at Cramer would like more clients like Ryan Technologies. And while I understand that companies often have a policy preventing them from giving referrals, we are hoping that would not be the case at Ryan. You might, in fact, be willing to refer us to associates who could use our services. As a leader in your field, a referral from you would carry extra meaning.

I will call next week to find out if you will be able to assist us. Either way, Cramer looks forward to our continued relationship with Ryan Technologies.

Sincerely

Robert Stone

Key Points

- You can start in a way that's a bit unusual as long as you gently remind your customer of your existing relationship and how much you value them.
- Point out the benefits of doing business with your company.
- Ask for a referral.
- Let the customer know when you will call and that, whatever their decision, your relationship does not depend on it.
- Give them an "out" in case their policy does not permit giving referrals.

5.5 Letter Offering Additional Complementary Products/Services

Situation Holland & Davis publishes a biannual directory of resources for the publishing industry entitled *The Publisher's Guidebook*. It is sold only by annual subscription. As soon as a new customer receives the first edition, Holland & Davis sends a letter offering a complementary product.

The Letter Dear Mr. Johnson (or Publisher's Guidebook Subscriber):

Thank you for your order.

I'm sure *The Publisher's Guidebook* will provide you with a wealth of valuable information that will save you both time and money—and put thousands of resources right at your fingertips.

The Publisher's Guidebook is indexed and organized to help you find all the information you need in minutes. It's like having a complete staff in your office, ready to find you the best source for any part of your company's publishing process.

And since, at Holland & Davis, we know what's really involved in turning that first draft into a perfect, finished product, we have a new, unique service to offer you. TPG References will allow *Publisher's Guide* subscribers *only* to access a database of references for each of the source listings in your *Guide*.

What does that mean to you?

It means that, after you've read through the listings for any source heading and pick the two or three who seem best for your needs—you can be sent by mail, or right on your own computer, references by actual TPG subscribers who have worked with the sources you're considering.

The choices you make can be both important and costly. *We want to help you make the right ones the first time!*

If you think TPG References would be an asset to you, call us at 1-800-555-0500 or send in the enclosed postpaid card for more information. You'll be glad you did!

Sincerely,

Editor

Key Points

- Thank your customer for the order.
- Remind buyers of a few of the key product features now available to them as a result of their initial purchase.
- Let customers know you have another product or service that is of special interest to them.
- Offer a few specifics about the new product. Use benefit-oriented copy so that customers understand what's in it for them.
- Ask customers to request more information if they are interested. Make it as easy as possible to get that information, either by phone or by an enclosed reply card.

5.6A Letter Offering Special Bonus for New Customer: Version 1

Situation The St. Louis Inn regularly sends follow-up letters to all first-time guests. The specifics of the letter are adapted to reflect the type of package or rate used by the guest—such as business rates, family or college visit specials, and the like. Alan Warwick has just completed a two-day stay at the Inn at a business rate. One week after his stay at the Inn, he will receive the following letter.

The Letter Dear Mr. Warwick:

It was a pleasure to have you as our guest at the St. Louis Inn. We certainly hope you enjoyed your stay—both at our hotel and in the St. Louis area!

Since you will hopefully be back in our area on business or pleasure in the near future, I thought you might want to know about the Inn's special frequent visitor program. It is designed for individuals like yourself who come to our area two or more times during the year.

The program includes discount rates based on your frequency of visits, plus a package of coupons offering you special prices at participating parking garages, car rentals, health clubs, restaurants, theatres, and more.

Please review the information I've enclosed and feel free to call me with any questions. Let us help make all your visits to our area as pleasant and economical as possible. If you choose not to take advantage of this offer, of course we look forward to providing you with our excellent service during your future visits to St. Louis.

Sincerely,

Concierge

Key Points

- Tell customers how happy you are to have them as customers.
- Explain the special bonus and why the customer qualifies.
- Let customers know that the bonus is a special invitation for them but that your good relationship does not depend on their taking advantage of your offer.
- Close by stating that you look forward to serving the customer in the future.

5.6B Letter Offering a Special Bonus for New Customer: Version 2

Situation A local vision center sends a letter to all new customers to thank them for their purchases and make a special offer to the customers and all their family members.

The Letter Dear Harold:

We want to take this opportunity to thank you for selecting Clearview Optical Center for your vision care needs.

Our special service number EYE-CARE is available for any questions you might have about your eyes or the vision care you received. Our experts are there every day between 9 A.M. and 5 P.M. to help you.

And, to show our appreciation for your recent purchase, we'd like to present you or any member of your family with a special offer of *$30.00 OFF* any purchase of a complete pair of prescription glasses. Come in to Clearview Optical Center any time until June 30 to take advantage of this offer.

Your continued confidence in us is the best incentive we could have to provide you and your family with the best eye care possible.

Sincerely,

Store Manager

P.S.: The new His and Her Lauren frames just arrived, plus several lines of sunglasses. Why not come over and take a look!

Key Points

- Thank customers for their patronage.
- Point out any special services you have that might interest them.
- Offer a special bonus as a direct result of their new customer status.
- Express concern for your customers.

5.7 Letter requesting Appointment for Sales Service Rep

Situation ClimaControl Air Conditioning Systems has sold a large cooling system to a warehouse and distribution facility. The purchase includes service visits to maintain the system's efficiency. The Service Manager needs to contact the customer to set up the first service inspection. An explanation of why this is necessary and what will happen next should be included in the letter.

The Letter Dear ______:

Congratulations on your purchase of a ClimaControl Central Air Conditioning System for your new warehouse and distribution center. You have purchased the finest product on the market today!

Although the system is designed to work efficiently and economically, it does require periodic maintenance to ensure peak performance. Part of your purchase price includes quarterly inspection vists during the first year of operation.

We would like to arrange the first of these visits for the week of April 2 if that is convenient for you. Your inspector, Barbara Gaines, will call you early next week to confirm the date.

As you know, there is no charge for the inspection and all repairs are covered by your maintenance contract. However, if filters need to be replaced, you will be billed for them.

At ClimaControl, our interest in you does not stop after the sale. Our policy of excellence in service lasts long after your system is installed.

Sincerely,

Service Manager

Key Points

- Offer a positive statement that reinforces your customer's decision to purchase your product.
- Explain why this service appointment is necessary.
- Provide details of what is needed so that the customer knows what to expect.
- To close, you can restate your policy of commitment to customer service.

5.8 Letter Stating Company Hours

Situation The Paper Warehouse sells a wide variety of paper products to both the public and the printing trade. Because customers are encouraged to save on delivery charges by picking up their orders, The Paper Warehouse always sends new customers a letter that includes the days and hours they are open.

The Letter Dear Mr. Bayless:

I wanted to personally thank you for your order for 20,000 A-7 Envelopes plus matching Note Cards, and welcome you as a new Paper Warehouse customer.

I believe you'll find that our range of products, low prices, and sincere desire to assist our customers will provide you with convincing reasons to call us for all your paper needs.

Did you know that if you pick up your order from our Seventh Street Warehouse, you'll not only save on the delivery charge, but be able to take advantage of our daily on-site specials?

We're open Monday through Friday from 7:30 A.M. to 4:30 P.M., and our staff is always available to help you place your order and load it into your vehicle.

We appreciate your business and look forward to supplying all your paper needs.

Sincerely,

Manager

Key Points

- Acknowledge the reader's new customer status.
- Offer additional information to reinforce the customer's decision to buy from your company.
- State your company hours and at least one reason why it is to the customer's advantage to buy from you. If there's no price advantage, mention other benefits. The personal attention of your trained staff, the ability to see your full range of merchandise, or the opportunity to compare different items are just a few.
- Repeat some words of appreciation for the customer's business and your anticipation of handling it in the future.

BONUS LETTER

The Clorox Company and their products are on everyone's household shelves. In addition to a strong line of products that live up to their promises, the company owes its success to a commitment to customer care and service.

The following new customer letter shows how they make relationship-building part of this commitment.

October 23, 1991

Dear :

Thank you very much for your recent purchase of Brita products from the Clorox Company.

We are committed to providing you with high-quality products, on-time delivery, and Superior Customer Service.

Please call us at our toll-free number 1-800-822-4101 between the hours of 7:00 a.m. to 3:30 p.m. (P.S.T.), and one of our Customer Service Representatives will be happy to place your order or assist you with any questions or problems.

Again, from all 5200 employees of The Clorox Company, thank you very much for choosing Clorox products!

Sincerely yours,

THE CLOROX COMPANY

Customer Service Manager

JAI:cma

5.9 Offering a Special Service Now Available to New Customers

Situation Tennis Shoppes is offering all buyers of a new Nelson 2000 Tennis Racket free participation in a one-day tennis clinic. A letter inviting these customers needs to be sent out.

The Letter Dear Tennis Enthusiast:

I have a very special offer for you—one available only to a select group of Tennis Shoppes customers. And it was your recent purchase of a Nelson 2000 Graphite racket that qualified you!

All Tennis Shoppes customers who have bought this brand-new racket are being invited to participate in a full-day tennis clinic at the The Graymore Tennis Club in Bedford Hills on Saturday, June 25. Nelson Sports Equipment has put together a superb staff of instructors to work with you on every part of your game so that you can get the most from your new purchase. But we've scheduled in some relaxation too. You'll be our guest at a sumptuous Graymore lunch buffet followed by a one-hour tennis exhibition game featuring two well-known players.

Sounds great, doesn't it? But you probably want to know why we're doing this and, yes, there is a reason. As our Tennis Shoppes salesperson told you, the Nelson 2000 racket is engineered using a brand-new technology. Nelson and Tennis Shoppes care about their customers and want their feedback on this new product.

Your only obligation for the day is to fill out a Nelson product questionnaire—and to have a really great time!

We hope you'll join us for this special day. Please call 314-555-4009 to reserve your spot. We're all looking forward to seeing you at Graymore!

Sincerely,

Dan Atkins
President

Key Points

- Offer your customers a special service and make it clear that their customer status is what entitles them to the offer.
- Explain the details of the offer.
- Make them feel really special about qualifying.

6 Follow-Up Letters

Any good sales organization knows that follow-up letters are a key step in its sales efforts—both to acquire customers and to keep them satisfied. Whether their purpose is to acknowledge, inform, remind, or resell, follow-up letters should be viewed as a required rather than an optional form of communication.

A well-written follow-up letter can motivate undecided buyers to buy. It can reassure sold customers of your continued concern for them, their needs, and their interests. It can bridge the way from your first contact to an eventual sale, or from your first sale to your next. A follow-up letter tells your customers that you live up to your promises—to provide the requested information, to make prompt delivery, to make your business transactions as problem-free as possible. And a follow-up letter can just tell your customers that you're thinking of them.

Following up with customers can also imply that your company is considerate, reliable, well-organized, and well-run. Thank-you notes and cards are another type of follow-up and can be sent after meetings, after sales, or on special occasions. They can make customers feel especially valued and appreciated.

Most sales do not occur after your first contact with a prospect. Often it takes several contacts with you or your product line before someone is ready to buy. And in today's competitive marketplace, even after one sale or more, your customer needs to keep being sold, time after time. This process of relationship building includes your staying in touch with the customer on a regular basis, whether there's a possible purchase on the horizon or not. Follow-up notes are one very important way of doing that.

Key Points:

- Follow-up letters should be a required step in your sales efforts and customer relations.
- A well-written follow-up letter can act as a motivator, a relationship strengthener, a bridge from sale to sale, an image-enhancer, and much more.
- Use follow-up letters for nonsales-specific occasions too. Send an article or piece of information relevant to a customer's interest, need, or earlier conversation.
- Sales rarely occur after a first contact with your prospective customer. Follow-up letters will not only help you meet its most obvious objective, but also allow you to remain in touch with your customers in many nonselling situations.
- A successful sales organization knows the importance of building relationships with customers. Follow-up letters can be a valuable part of that process.

6.1 After the First Order

Situation Robert Berne has recently purchased a Maxwell Compact Disk Player and 12-CD "Music Library" from Hart's store. At the time of his purchase, he is asked to fill out a survey card about his musical preferences. The president of Hart's then sends him this follow-up letter.

The Letter Dear Mr. Berne:

I'd like to congratulate you on your recent purchase of a Maxwell Compact Disk Player. Its state-of-the-art sound quality should provide you with listening pleasure for many years to come.

I would also like to thank you for participating in our "Musical Choices of the 90's" survey at the time you made your purchase.

Enclosed you will find the new *Cool Jazz* CD, which is our way of saying thanks for your recent purchase and assistance in our survey.

Once again, we hope you enjoy your Maxwell Compact Disk Player and the music you've selected. And remember, when you're ready to expand your music library, Hart's has the largest selection of CDs in the New City area—and special Discount Picks every week!

Sincerely,

President

P.S.: If you'd like a copy of our survey results, it will be available FREE at all Hart's stores after August 15. Stop in and pick one up!

Key Points

- Thank customers for their recent purchase, and remind them of how they they will benefit from their choice.
- Make a special offer, now that they are your customers. This could be a gift, a "special," a piece of valuable information that is now relevant, or anything that expresses how you value your customers.
- Again, state your appreciation for their patronage and your hope for future business.

6.2 After a Lost Sale

Situation Bartwell & Eaves, an organizational development consulting firm, finds out that they have lost a training contract to a competitor. One of the partners writes a letter to the customer to express disappointment over the lost sale and to keep the door open for future business.

The Letter Dear ______:

Although I admit I was disappointed to hear you had chosen The Morgan Group instead of Bartwell & Eaves for your current supervisory training needs, I very much appreciate your honesty. Your willingness to explain the reasons for this decision makes you unique in my book!

This information has already proven to be extremely helpful to all of us at B&E. Of course, I was also glad to hear that, despite this decision, you feel we might be able to work together in the future.

I will put the feedback you gave me into action and begin work on a program proposal for you, to be ready for implementation by fall of 1993, if approved.

Thank you again for all your valuable input. I still believe that Bartwell & Eaves can provide you with a custom-designed program that will meet all your specific needs and requirements. I hope that one day soon we'll be able to work together.

Sincerely,

Partner

Key Points

- Acknowledge that your company has lost a sale.
- If you know why, you can state the reason in the most positive way possible to leave the door open for future business.
- If there is a specific timetable or deadline for your next selling opportunity, mention when customers will hear from you next and how you plan to make your product or service a better match for their needs.
- Thank customers for their time and input, if appropriate. Express your anticipation of future business.

6.3 After a Catalog/New Product Announcement Is Sent

Situation L'Orange, a beauty aids manufacturer, has developed a new nailcare product. A product announcement is sent to beauty salons and distributors. One month later, they send the following letter to the prospective buyers who did not respond to the original announcement.

The Letter Dear ______:

Last month, we sent you information about our brand new nailcare product, DURANAIL. Three years of research, design, and extensive testing have shown us that DURANAIL will make a noticeable difference in your clients' nails with only three weeks' use. And, for a majority of women, long-term use will grow those long, healthy, flexible, yet strong nails they've always wanted, but have never been able to achieve naturally.

You've probably heard similar claims before from other products—and perhaps you've been disappointed in the results. But DURANAIL is different! Different enough that your customers will prove us right by wanting to make DURANAIL use a regular part of their nailcare—both in your salon and at home.

And to prove this, L'Orange is sending you a FREE box of samples—*three weeks supply for one dozen trial users.* So you won't have to take our word for DURANAIL's reliability before you place your first order.

Your sample package should arrive this week. A L'Orange representative will be in touch with you next month to hear about the results. Of course, we're also available to answer any questions you might have about DURANAIL and any of our other L'Orange products. We're always happy to hear from our customers and assist them in any way possible.

Sincerely,

President

Key Points

- Remind the customer that earlier information was sent to them and what it was about. Highlight one or two of the most important features originally mentioned about your product(s).
- Focus on your product's most important benefit to your customer or to the end user.
- In this follow-up, you can offer free samples, trial usage, a free visit, or any other incentive to get these customers to try your new product.
- Let your customers know what will happen next. Also remind them of their special status as customers and how you value their relationship.

6.4 After a Customer Visit to a Company Store

Situation John's Sporting Goods Stores regularly collects names of customers who visit their stores. In addition to a name and address, John's staff asks store visitors which types of products they are most interested in. They are then able to send out personalized follow-up letters like the one following.

The Letter Dear Mr. Jergen:

When you visited the Danville branch of John's Sporting Goods four weeks ago, you told us that, while you participate in many sports, tennis is your favorite.

Because of that, we thought you would be interested in our new line of state-of-the-art Munson Rackets, considered by experts to be the racket "Technology of the 90's." Made from a combination of graphite and fiberglass, the Munson 5000 series allows for added control plus significantly increased power—an ideal combination for any level player.

The Munson 5000 line will be available in all our stores as of April 1, just in time for the spring season. And we're inviting you to stop by and see what all the excitement is about!

To thank you for shopping at John's Sporting Goods Stores—and making a trip down to see us. We've also enclosed a special discount coupon entitling you to three cans of Munson all-surface tennis balls for the price of one. That's a $5.98 savings!

We look forward to seeing you again soon!

Sincerely,

Store Manager

P.S.: Your discount coupon can be redeemed at any of our locations. So swing into spring at your nearest John's Sporting Goods!

Key Points

- Acknowledge the customer's visit to your store. Mention at least one piece of personal information that ties into the reason for your letter.
- Tell customers why you are writing. If the letter's objective is to get them to visit your store again, provide just enough information to pique their interest.
- It is a good idea to use a specific date or deadline, to add a sense of urgency to the offer.
- If appropriate, you might also want to offer an incentive with a stated value to the customer, such as a discount coupon, or a free or discounted bonus.
- Since this is a personal letter, you can let customers know you're looking forward to their next visit.

6.5 After a Prospect Visits the Trade Show Booth

Situation At the recent Premium Show, BCA Specialty Gifts asked each person visiting their booth to sign a visitor's log. Whenever possible, the sales rep attending to the visitor also noted which items or types of items the prospect was interested in. Two weeks after the show, follow-up letters were sent to all the people whose names were in the log.

The Letter Dear Mr. Reisman:

Thanks so much for stopping by our booth at the recent Premium Show in Las Vegas. I hope you liked our Wheel of Fortune theme and were one of the prize winners. But even if you didn't have time to participate, I'm glad you were able to take our new catalog with you to review in the office with your staff.

We've just added a new group of items that might interest you, and I've enclosed sales sheets that clearly illustrate them. I think you'll agree that this is a very handsome desk set—and each piece can be handled separately if you want to give away only one or assemble a smaller set.

I know you said that flexibility was one of the features most important to you, and this set has seven pieces to choose from. Other finishes are also available, which would vary the price as well as the look.

Let me know if this or any of our other catalog items fits your needs. I'll be happy to provide you with whatever other details you require. And, if none of these seems just right, I will keep you in mind as we add new products.

Sincerely,

Account Manager

Key Points

- Thank customers for their visit to your exhibit booth, and include one or two specifics to help remember you. Also mention anything that might have been taken from the booth as a sample.
- Tell the visitor about a new item or special offer—perhaps something specific that was not available at the time of the show.
- If possible, show visitors that you remember something specific about their companies, their needs, or your conversation. It will help them remember you and make them feel special.
- Keep your sales pitch as low keyed as possible. Your objective is to extend this new relationship beyond the trade show itself.
- If the customer expressed significant interest, set a time when you will telephone.

6.6 After a Visit to a Company Plant

Situation The chief engineer for an exercise clothing company has just visited a contract manufacturer's plant for an equipment and quality control inspection. The head of manufacturing for the plant facility writes a follow-up letter to the engineer to confirm the results of this visit.

The Letter Dear ______:

I'm glad you were able to visit our Huntsville manufacturing facility last Thursday for a machinery inspection and quality control procedures check.

I hope you were as satisfied with our new automated tagging equipment as we have been. We expect it to save significant time in our postproduction operations and help get your orders packed and on our trucks within 24 hours of completion.

John Hawkins relayed your recommendation regarding our sampling check. I understand that you expect us to inspect 10 percent of all finished piece goods rather than our usual 5 percent. This new procedure will go into effect on Monday when the first run of garments from your order #T3825 is finished.

We see no problem in meeting your November 1 request for delivery. Please let me know if I can be of any further assistance.

Sincerely,

Director of Manufacturing

Key Points

- Express your pleasure at their plant visit and mention the specific reasons for that visit.
- Point out some positive feature or capability about your facility that they would have appreciated.
- If your customer has issued any instructions regarding an order as a result of this visit, put it in writing to prevent possible miscommunication.
- Offer your continued assistance, and welcome additional visits, if appropriate.

6.7 After a First Sales Call

Situation Mary Collins, a new sales representative, has just completed a meeting with Gary Evans, the President of Johnson Controls, Inc. a long-time customer. A letter is sent to review the meeting and to help build the new salesperson-client relationship.

The Letter Dear Gary:

Thank you for the time you gave me today to meet you and learn about Johnson Controls. I certainly found our discussion informative.

As promised, I have enclosed the engineering report on the microvalve that you were interested in. It has been used successfully in projects such as yours and can possibly be the answer to your humidity control problem.

If you have technical questions about the microvalve, please call Hank DeLoft at our headquarters. I've alerted him to expect your call.

I've also enclosed two recent articles from *Control Engineering News* that I think you will find pertinent.

I want you to know that I am preparing the quotation that we discussed and will have it in your hands before the June 22 deadline. I'm sure you'll find our capabilities as well as the bottom line most attractive.

Again, thank you for the opportunity to meet with you and to quote the Pacific Basin project. I'm looking forward to working with you and Johnson Controls in the future.

Sincerely,

Mary Collins

Key Points

- Thank the customer for the meeting.
- Review what was discussed and what actions will be taken next.
- When possible, offer something extra (information, samples, referrals, or the like) as a means of showing your interest in the customer and your desire to build a strong relationship.
- Specifically state what the customer is to expect next.
- Close by expressing your expectation to do business with the customer.

6.8 Confirmation of an Order

Situation Pretty Papers, a gift wrap manufacturer, has received a telephone order from a Mr. Harvey, who needs the merchandise in time for the upcoming holiday season. The seller needs to confirm all the specifics of the order in writing, leaving enough time to make changes if they do not agree with the customer's records.

The Letter Dear Mr. Harvey:

This confirms your order #435 placed on November 12 by phone. The order includes the following items:

Quantity	*Size*	*Style*	*Description*	*$ Per Roll*
2	60′	1800	Sunflowers	$102.80
3	60 ′	423H	Tuxedo Park	$116.80
1	30′	5600	Glossy Red	$ 92.00
1	30′	5603	Glossy Green	$ 92.00
4	30′	5602	Glossy White	$ 92.00
1	60′ 1″	400	White Ribbon	$ 32.60
1	60′ ½″	402	White Ribbon	$ 21.00
1	60′ ½″	408	Plaid Ribbon	$ 27.80

I understand that you need this order at least one month prior to the Spring holidays. We can promise delivery the week of March 2. Call me as soon as you receive this if any of the information does not match your records or if the delivery date needs to be changed.

Thanks so much for selecting Pretty Papers for your wrapping needs. We're expecting our new summer patterns in soon, and samples will be sent to you as quickly as possible. In the meantime, let us know if there's any other way we can assist you.

Sincerely,

Order Department

Key Points

- Be specific right away so that it is clear to the customer exactly what you are confirming. Make sure you include the purchase order number, if there is one, and the date the order was placed, as well as all the items ordered and their prices.
- If the customer makes a special request regarding any aspect of the order, give it special mention in your confirmation. Ask the customer to notify you if your information does not match his or hers.
- Thank the customer for the order and express interest in future business.

6.9 Confirmation of Appointment

Situation Gumbel's home decorating service sends out a written confirmation for every appointment made. It states not only the time and day of the appointment but also the areas of the home to be discussed. If possible, the name of the scheduled representative is mentioned with one or two of his/her credentials to make the customer more comfortable about the appointment.

The Letter

Dear Mr. and Mrs. Roth:

This letter confirms your appointment for Tuesday, January 11, 7:30 P.M. with Gumbel's Decorate-at-Home Service.

Marcie Brewer is scheduled to work with you on your living and dining room remodeling plans. She will be specifically bringing catalogs, fabric, and flooring samples for those rooms. If you have other areas of the home you'd like to discuss, let us know so that she can be sure to have everything with her that you might want to see.

You may be interested to know that Marcie was the winner of the 1988 and 1989 Young Decorator's Award offered at our annual Spring Designer Showcase. I know you'll enjoy working with her to create a very special area of your home.

Sincerely,

Home Services Manager

Key Points

- Confirm your appointment mentioning, all the specifics.
- If the representative has not already been introduced, name the rep in the letter.
- Review what will happen at this appointment, and advise the customer if he or she needs to do anything in preparation.
- Offer a positive piece of information about your representative or the appointment results.

6.10 Confirmation of a Delivery Schedule

Situation A written confirmation of a delivery schedule is regularly sent to all Texasline customers. This ensures that customers are aware of the delivery dates and times as they get closer. All the details are clearly spelled out, with a phone number for each party to call if a problem arises. This type of letter should be kept as short, simple, and specific as possible.

The Letter Dear Joe:

Thank you again for your order for 6 truckloads of Texasline rice, long grain, 100# bags. We understand that you are unable to take this quantity in one delivery and would like 3 truckload drops made over the next three months.

The following is our delivery schedule for this order. Please let us know immediately if you will be unable to accept delivery on these days or times.

Delivery #1—May 8, P.M. (between 1 P.M. and 5 P.M.)

Delivery #2—July 10, A.M. (between 7:30 A.M. and noon)

Delivery #3—September 6, P.M.

Our drivers have your name and number, and will phone you to reconfirm approximately three days before arrival.

Sincerely,

Key Points

- Thank your customer for the order. Restate the delivery request.
- Let the customer know if he or she needs to take any further action.
- Describe in detail your plans for delivery.
- Supply any other information your customer may need.

6.11 Confirmation of Receipt of Signed Contract

Situation Top Hat Cleaning Service has just taken on a new customer. The owner of Top Hat wants to acknowledge receipt of the signed contract and review when work will start. Since any discussion of services or prices would have taken place prior to a final contract, a short note is appropriate.

The Letter Dear Ms. Moore:

Thank you for promptly returning your signed copy of Top Hat's cleaning service contract for 1992. We're sure you'll be extremely pleased with your decision to use our firm.

Our first service appointment is scheduled for Tuesday, January 2 at 5 A.M. and we expect to be out of your offices by 8 A.M.—before most of your staff arrives.

If you need to speak to me directly, or if any special arrangements need to be made, my assistant or I can always be reached on our beeper #742-3485.

Sincerely,

President

Key Points

- Thank your customer for the signed contract. Reinforce their choice to work with you.
- State your next step in fulfilling this contract.
- Even if contact between the two of you is not necessary now that the contract is signed, let the customer know that you will continue to be available if needed.

6.12 After No Response to Several Contacts

Situation Smith Marine Supply has had its catalog printed by Xpress Lithographers four times in the last two years. Mark Newhouse, Xpress's account executive, has not heard from Smith Marine in six months. Smith Marine is due to print another catalog, but has not returned Mark's phone calls. Mark decides to send a letter hoping to reestablish communications with this important client.

The Letter Dear ______:

Have we done something wrong?

Over the last two years, we have printed your catalog on four separate occasions. Each time, you expressed satisfaction with the job. It's been six months since your last printing, and we have not heard from you. Frankly, we are very concerned!

Your account is very important to Xpress and we don't want to lose it. We can only think of two reasons why you're not printing with us now.

First, we did something wrong. If we did, we're sorry. And we'd appreciate finding out what it was so that we can correct our error. We know we can satisfy you. Please give us a chance.

Or . . .

Second, you got a better price. Printing is very competitive, and we understand your need to keep costs down. If you received a better price, that's great. But why not give us a chance to meet it . . . or even beat it. You'll get an excellent price from us, along with our top-notch quality and concerned customer service.

As in your business, we need to know when we're off the mark. Please help us to serve our customers better by telling us where we came up short.

I'll call you next Friday morning to see if Xpress can be of service to Smith Marine.

Thank you very much for your time.

Sincerely,

Mark Newhouse

Key Points

- Open with an attention-getting question or statement.
- Explain the situation as you see it.
- Express your keen interest in working with the customer.
- Tell customers that their business is important to you and that you are eager to reestablish the relationship.
- Inform customers of exactly what action you will take next.

7

Letters to Handle Justified Complaints

When an error has been made that causes customer dissatisfaction, it is the responsibility of the company to quickly and fairly make the matter right.

Nothing shows your commitment to customer service excellence better than a fast response to a justified complaint. Your customers know that they have been wronged and expect immediate satisfaction. Anything less than that will cause your customers to think twice before ordering from you again.

When your company has made a mistake, say so. Honesty is not just the best policy, it is the only policy. By being honest, you earn your customer's respect. But do not get involved in long, complicated explanations. Explain your point of view directly and then put your attention on showing the customer how you will make up for your mistake.

Often, to keep a customer after making an error, you'll have to "go the extra mile"—offer the customer free merchandise or services, special discounts on future orders, or a gift. A bouquet of flowers or a teddy bear can make a friend of even the most disgruntled customer. It isn't necessary to spend a lot of money, but it is necessary to show your sincere desire to make amends.

Your response should be mailed immediately. When possible, send it out by overnite courier or Express Mail. Show your customers by your actions that you are truly sorry. And assure them that steps have been taken to make sure there is no repeat of the error in the future. Always end by restating your apology and expressing your expectation of future business. Offer customers an opportunity for additional discussion if they are still unsatisfied with your response.

Key Points

- Your immediate response to a justified complaint is necessary and expected.
- Admit your mistake and then tell the customer how you will make things right.
- Offer an appropriate token to show the customer that you wish to make things right.
- When possible, send your letter by overnight delivery. State that the mistake will not happen again, and express your expectation of future business with the customer.

7.1 Response to a Complaint over a Billing Error

Situation A company has received a customer letter showing a billing error in a current invoice and requesting a correction. Upon checking, the company finds that the customer is correct. A letter must be sent to resolve the problem and apologize for the error.

The Letter Dear ______:

We've received your letter of June 8 requesting an adjustment for a billing error. After reviewing your order, we find that you are absolutely correct—an error has been made.

We apologize for the mistake. While there are no excuses for such an error, when thousands of orders are processed each month, an error or two will occur. We're so sorry that your order was billed incorrectly.

Attached is a correct invoice for the amount of $673.45. Please discard any previous invoices. Our Accounting Department has been notified of the correction and has made the necessary adjustments to your account.

Again, we're sorry for any inconvenience this may have caused you.

Sincerely,

Credit Manager

Key Points

- Tell the customer why you are writing. Be candid about the fact that your company has made a mistake.
- Apologize for your mistake. If there is a reason that can be given briefly, include it—but only as an explanation, not an excuse.
- Explain how the situation will be resolved.
- It is appropriate to again express your apologies for the mistake.

7.2 Response to a Complaint over a Continued Billing Error

Situation A customer has written to complain that an error in billing has not been corrected, even though the customer notified the billing department a month earlier. A letter is sent to the customer apologizing for the mistake and offering a small gift in way of an apology.

The Letter Dear ______:

I am writing you to apologize twice.

First, we apologize for the billing error that was reflected in your September statement. You were charged for three Elegante Place Settings at $72 each, when in fact you ordered two. An adjustment to your account has been made and you will see a credit of $72 applied as of November 1.

Second, we apologize for not correcting this error on your October statement after you notified us of the mistake. Due to a clerical oversight, no credit was issued.

At Garfield's we hate to make errors. Two errors made to a good customer like you is totally unacceptable. We are taking measures now to ensure that this never occurs again.

In the meantime, please accept our apologies and the $100 gift certificate enclosed. Hopefully, it will make up in some small way for the inconvenience that you have suffered.

Sincerely,

Key Points

- Apologize for the errors. Since two mistakes were made, you should express your embarrassment and dissatisfaction with your performance.
- State that errors such as these are unusual and that you are taking steps to prevent their recurrence.
- Explain that the matter has finally been resolved.
- Offer a small token to appease the customer.

7.3 Response to a Complaint over a Computer Error

Situation A customer's payment was not credited to his account due to a computer error. A letter is sent to the customer explaining the situation and indicating that the appropriate adjustment has been made.

The Letter Dear Mr. Whitelaw:

We have received your letter, dated August 13, indicating that you were not credited for a payment that you made to resolve invoice number 12234.

We are sorry to admit that, in addition to your letter, we have received over one hundred others. Upon investigation, we discovered that all payments entered on June 23 were not credited to the proper accounts due to a computer error.

Thank you for making us aware of this unfortunate mistake. We have corrected your account to reflect your payment. It now shows no balance due.

We want to apologize for the error. In this age of high technology, computers provide an invaluable service. However, when a computer glitch occurs, control is often lost. We are currently taking steps to prevent an error like this from occurring again in the future.

We greatly appreciate your understanding and patience.

Sincerely,

Accounts Receivable Manager

Key Points

- Explain the situation as you understand it. Explain what happened as simply as possible since most people do not have technical backgrounds.
- Tell the customer that you have corrected the error and apologize for the mistake.
- Promise to do better in the future.

BONUS LETTER

This letter, sent by Quill Corporation to smooth over a problem experienced by a customer, shows their genuine appreciation and concern for the customer. In addition to the responsive words, they include a small gift as a "reminder that you should expect only the best from Quill."

Not only has Quill gone out of its way to satisfy the customer, it has also challenged itself to keep its standards high.

QUILL®
CORPORATION

Corporate Headquarters
100 Schelter Rd.
Lincolnshire, Illinois 60069-3621
Phone 708-634-6690
Fax 708-634-6699

May 15, 1991

Mr. John Doe
ABC Company
501 Main St.
Anywhere, USA

Dear Mr. Doe:

One of our favorite sayings is:

"No one has a divine right to survive and prosper. It is a right that must be earned day in and day out."

We intend to earn that right by constantly serving your needs in the finest manner possible and by making Quill the most convenient and satisfying way for you to shop.

We sincerely regret the problem you recently experienced with us and have done everything possible to set the record straight. If everything has not been resolved to your 100 percent satisfaction, please let me know. We want to make it right!

Please accept this mug as a constant reminder that you should expect only the best from Quill. We've set our standards high, and we expect to be held to those standards.

Sincerely,

Tom Smith
Service Analysis Coordinator

7.4 Response to a Complaint over a Shipping Error

Situation A customer has placed a rush order with a distributor to fulfill an important order. Part of the instructions were that the order must ship on a particular date. The distributor met the deadline but shipped an incomplete order. The customer called to complain and threatened to take its business elsewhere. The distributor sends a quick written response by overnight mail.

The Letter Dear ______:

I am writing to apologize for the error that was made in shipping your order #228 placed on October 20.

I was just informed that, instead of shipping 11 cartons of Aqua Fresh Pool Cleaner, only 6 cartons were sent. I am also aware that this was a special order and that the product was needed immediately.

We offer no excuse for the mistake. An error was certainly made. We are at fault. All that we can do now is try to correct the problem as quickly as possible.

I am sending you by overnight delivery 7 cartons of Aqua Fresh—5 cartons to complete the order and 2 extra free cartons to show that we are truly sorry for our error.

Naturally, we will pay the overnight shipping charges.

You have always been an excellent customer. We appreciate your business and want to keep it. We will do all that is possible to guarantee that all your future orders are shipped exactly as you instruct.

Again, we are truly sorry for the mistake.

Sincerely,

Sales Manager

Key Points

- Apologize immediately.
- Explain the situation to show that you understand why the customer is upset.
- Detail how you will correct the problem. Offer something extra to make amends for your mistake.
- Tell customers how important their business is to you and express your commitment to satisfying their future needs.

7.5 Response to a Complaint over Defective Merchandise

Situation A good customer has placed an order for custom-printed business forms. The forms were printed incorrectly and shipped. Now the printer must resolve the problem and keep this important customer satisfied. A letter is sent explaining what the printer intends to do.

The Letter Dear ______:

We received your letter requesting return authorization for your order No. EDF-987. We are sorry to learn that the three-part forms were incorrectly printed with your information appearing on only the top two sheets.

We are immediately issuing a request for UPS to pick up the merchandise for return to our warehouse. We are also placing a rush order for this merchandise and can promise delivery to you by next Thursday, August 4.

We apologize for the printing error. Your order should have been checked and the mistake discovered before it was shipped to you.

In checking your customer records, I found that you ordered from us over a dozen times last year. Your confidence in us is much appreciated, and it makes us even more embarrassed for this mistake. We hope you will not hold it against us.

We will do all we can to make sure this does not happen again.

Thank you for your loyalty and continued business.

Sincerely,

Customer Service Manager

P.S.: You will not be charged for this order. It is our way of showing how sorry we are for the error.

Key Points

- Show your understanding of the error and apologize for it.
- Quickly explain what steps you are taking to resolve the problem. Make sure it is evident that you are taking special care.
- Restate your apology and expectation that this will not occur again.
- If possible, offer the shipment at no cost, reduced cost, or with free shipping.

BONUS LETTER

The name Campbell's is as American as... chicken noodle soup. And Campbell Soup Company has long been acknowledged as a leader in quality control.

When a customer expresses concern about a product, an apology letter is immediately sent, along with a promise to look further into the situation. The company's rigid quality control procedures are detailed to reassure the customer. And, of course, the customer is reimbursed for the cost of the product in question.

Campbell Soup Company

May 23, 1991

Dear

Thank you for contacting us about Campbell's Tomato Soup. We are very sorry that you had this experience and appreciate your taking the time to share your concern with us.

Our aim is to provide you with products of consistently high quality, time after time. To that end, we employ many procedures in the manufacturing process to protect and maintain product standards. For example, each ingredient we buy has to meet our strict specifications for wholesomeness and is inspected several times before being combined into a finished product. The ingredients are carefully protected during processing. Employees stationed on each production line continually check the product, and generally, electronic and mechanical aids have been installed to help our trained employees maintain wholesomeness in our products.

On the basis of your report, I am asking our quality control and production people to investigate how the defect you reported could have occurred and to review their procedures accordingly.

I also would like to reimburse you for the cost of the product that caused your concern. We invite you to use the enclosed coupons to try this product again or some other Campbell product if you prefer.

We value your opinion. Consumers such as you help us continue to work toward better products.

Sincerely,

CONSUMER RELATIONS, CAMDEN, NEW JERSEY 08103-1701

7.6 Response to a Complaint over Damaged Merchandise

Situation A customer received a shipment of insulated windows in damaged condition. The shipment was refused. The supplier must immediately address the problem and offer a solution. A letter is sent to explain that the supplier is not at fault for the damage but has taken responsibility for resolving the problem.

The Letter Dear ______:

Thank you for alerting us about the shipment of damaged goods.

We are sorry for the inconvenience you have suffered and are taking steps right now to remedy the problem. After investigation, we have discovered that the ClearProtect Windows were damaged in transit. They did leave our factory in perfect condition.

We have placed an order with our distribution center, and they promise to reship your windows within four working days. Therefore you can expect delivery on or about July 19.

Again, I apologize for any trouble you have experienced. I will call you on July 20 to make sure that your new shipment arrived satisfactorily.

Sincerely,

General Manager

Key Points

- Apologize for the problem, even if it is not your fault.
- Describe how the problem will be resolved.
- If you are not at fault, say so without putting blame elsewhere.
- Tell the customer exactly when to expect the new shipment.
- If you offer to follow up, make sure that you do.

BONUS LETTER

Warner Lambert, the manufacturer of so many products that we have learned to rely upon, is the producer of Listerine Antiseptic. When a customer writes of trouble with a bottle, the company quickly thanks the customer for writing, apologizes for the inconvenience, and explains how such a defect could occur. The customer is also offered a coupon to be used to replace the damaged bottle. An extract of the letter follows.

> It is always a pleasure, ______, to hear from our valued consumers, but we are sorry to learn of the unfortunate experience you report having with a bottle of Listerine Antiseptic.
>
> We assure you we have exceedingly rigid inspections, both at the plant of our bottle suppliers and again at our laboratories where this product is made. In spite of these precautions, bottles with very minute deviations occasionally pass through.
>
> It is also possible a severe shock or blow during shipment weakened a spot in the glass. The increased pressure due to the increase in temperature may have forced the glass at this spot to give way. Heat causes expansion. Expansion causes pressure. If a bottle has been filled too close to the top, leaving insufficient expansion space, it will break at its weakened point.
>
> We apologize for any inconvenience this incident may have caused you and are enclosing a coupon redeemable for a bottle of Listerine Antiseptic. Please accept it with our best wishes.

7.7 Response to a Complaint over Employee Rudeness

Situation While flying to Chicago, Jon Goodman was verbally abused by an air attendant. He wrote a letter of complaint to the airline. Air America has responded to Jon to answer his complaint and to try to keep him as a customer.

The Letter Dear Mr. Goodman:

I am writing to offer our apology for the rudeness shown you by one of our employees on your flight to Chicago. There is no excuse whatsoever for any employee treating a customer with anything less than the utmost respect.

We'd like to thank you for bringing this matter to our attention. By doing so, we are able to take action to ensure that this type of behavior does not occur again.

Specifically, Tom Evans has been dismissed because of this incident and the attitude problem that it represents.

Again, we are so sorry that you had this unpleasant experience while flying with us. I'd like to assure you, however, that Air America employees are considered to be among the most considerate and courteous in the industry. Your experience was certainly an exception.

We sincerely hope that you will give Air America another chance to prove how concerned our employees are with our passengers' satisfaction. I'd like to offer you a 2-for-1 pass so that you and a guest can experience the kind of quality service we are known for.

Again, please accept our apology.

Sincerely,

Customer Service Manager

Key Points

- Acknowledge the complaint. Cite a specific aspect or incident so that your letter addresses the problem in a personal manner.
- Describe what actions have been taken to resolve the problem and satisfy the customer.
- Offer an incentive to the customer to continue using your service.
- Close by apologizing a second time.

7.8 Response to a Complaint over Being Given Incorrect Buying Information

Situation Smith and Potter Tax Services purchased self-sealing corrugated mailing envelopes to use for all their tax returns. The sales rep from Duval Office Supplies told them that Envelope #15 would hold up to 48 pages of 8½ × 11 20# paper, which would satisfy S&P's standard requirements. When the envelopes were received, S&P found that the inner dimensions of the envelopes are actually 8½ × 10⅜ and do not accommodate the tax returns. A letter of complaint is sent and Duval must resolve the problem.

The Letter Dear ______:

You're absolutely right! The #15 envelopes that you ordered are meant to hold 8 × 10 materials or smaller. Unfortunately, you were given the wrong information when you ordered. The correct product for your needs would be our #20 Envelopes, which are designed to fit 8½ × 11-inch documents.

We are terribly sorry for the misinformation. Your sales rep is new with us, and we've now made sure he thoroughly understands all our product lines.

We'd like to resolve your problem immediately. The ten cases of #15 envelopes can be replaced with #20s. Just give us a call with your ok and our driver will schedule delivery. And, to make up for your inconvenience, we'll include two additional cases at no charge.

Thank you for your patience and understanding.

Sincerely,

Vice President of Sales

Key Points

- Take responsibility right away for your mistake. You might want to let the customer know you've taken steps so that this mistake cannot happen again.
- Tell the customer how you plan to resolve the problem.
- Thank customers for their patience and understanding.

7.9 Response to a Complaint over a Lack of Promptness in Correcting a Problem

Situation The customer service manager of Gladstone Resorts has written the following response to a customer complaint. The customer's cancellation refund has taken three months to be processed—much longer than he feels is necessary.

The Letter Dear Mr. Harrison:

Your letter of September 23 has just been brought to my attention. I am very sorry to hear that it took almost three months for you to receive a refund for the cancelled hotel reservations.

As customer service manager, my job is to make sure that all Gladstone Resort customers receive courteous, prompt attention to their problems and special needs.

You are justified in feeling that three months is much too long to credit your credit card account. Once we are notified of a cancellation, it should only take a few days to process your refund.

While we have no excuse for the delay, we assure you that normally refunds are processed much faster. Because of an error, your account unfortunately was neglected.

As you can see from the enclosed credit memo, your account has now been credited for the full amount. I've also enclosed a voucher for a free night's stay at Gladstone to express how sorry we are about the delay. Besides hotel room accommodations, you'll receive a free breakfast for two. We hope you'll enjoy your visit to our resort.

Again, thank you for bringing this matter to my attention. I will take measures to see that this oversight does not happen again.

Sincerely,

Customer Service Manager

Key Points

- Offer your apologies for your company's slow handling of the customer's problem.
- Empathize with your customer's feelings, and agree that the problem should have been handled differently.
- Don't make excuses. You may, however, want to show that this instance was an exception to your usual policy. Or you may want to briefly explain why your policy lapsed.
- Tell the customer how your company has rectified the situation. If you are able, offer an extra inducement to assure further business with this customer.

7.10 Response to a Complaint over a Promise Not Kept

Situation One of the most difficult complaint letters to answer is for a promise not kept. Customers rely on the word and good intentions of their suppliers. When a promise is made, they expect it to be kept. The only way to satisfy a customer in such a situation is to sincerely express your apology and state that you accept all the blame. Don't be afraid to express how badly you feel about letting the customer down. Make a generous offer to make up for the harm caused.

The Letter

Dear ______:

Please accept my apologies. . . .

You are 100 percent right. When you placed your order for invitations on December 6, you explained that your party would be held on January 25 and that you needed the invitations by January 3.

I promised you that we could and would meet that deadline.

I can only imagine how upset you must have been when the invitations did not arrive on January 3 and it took until the 10th for you to get them. By then, it was too late.

I feel especially bad because it was my promise that was broken. I do want to assure you that I sincerely believed that we would be able to deliver on January 3. Unfortunately, our press broke down and the repairperson was out of town. That delay ruined the schedule for you and others.

Naturally, there is no charge for the invitations and we have already credited your invoice. To show you how sorry I am, I'd like to offer you free invitations for your next party or event. And I'll do everything possible to make sure we meet your dates.

Again, I'm so sorry for the inconvenience you experienced.

Sincerely,

Sales Representative

Key Points

- Immediately express your genuine regrets.
- Explain the situation so that the customer knows you realize that you broke your promise.
- Tell the customer that you did not intentionally mislead him/her.
- Suggest something that you can do to diminish the harm.

8

Letters to Handle Unjustified Complaints

Customer complaints . . . unfortunately, you can't run a business without getting them. Even the most successful, well-run business gets its share. What's really important is how you handle each complaint. And when a complaint turns out to be unjustified because the customer is at fault, the provider of the product or service must be extra careful.

Contrary to the adage, customers are not always right. But arguing with a customer or assigning blame does nothing to positively resolve the problem or solidify your relationship.

Regardless of who is at fault, your focus should be on satisfactorily resolving the problem for your customers. Even though you do not want to blame them, or focus on the fact that *you* did nothing wrong, you do want to be honest about what has happened. To avoid future problems, you may need to acknowledge the truth about the complaint. In each instance, evaluate the specifics of the situation, keeping your focus on the best possible resolution.

Key Points

- Expect to have some customer complaints, no matter how well you run your business.
- Even if your customer is entirely at fault, avoid arguing or assigning blame.
- In a nonaccusatory way, try to be honest and straightforward about the situation that led to the complaint.
- Keep your focus on solving the problem and on educating the customer so that the problem does not happen again.

8.1 Response to a Complaint over Incorrect Merchandise

Situation A customer has complained that one of the items received in her order is not what she requested. While company policy should exist that would dictate the customer service response, it is important in today's service-oriented market to try to accommodate your customers as much as possible.

The Letter Dear Ms. Baines:

I have now been able to check our order records and shipping manifest for your order of June 12.

In your attached letter, you stated that one item in the package you received did not match your original request. You also asked for return authorization for that portion of your order.

As you can see from the copies I've enclosed, the items specified on your purchase order do match those on the packing slip.

However, we do want our customers to be completely satisfied with any item ordered from us. So, as long as your return pick-up is arranged within 14 days of order receipt and the merchandise is still in its shipping carton, we'll be happy to take it back. Our Return Authorization Department can be reached between 9 and 5 at 1-800-555-3000.

We're glad we were able to assist you and look forward to serving you in the future.

Sincerely,

Manager

Key Points

- Restate the specifics of the complaint. Enclose the customer's letter, if possible.
- Tell the customer what your search has uncovered. If there is a simple reason for the problem, it should be explained.
- If the customer is at fault, there's no need to take the blame yourself, or to focus on the fact that they are in error—as long as there is an amenable solution to the problem.
- Offer whatever solution is available to satisfy the customer.
- Express your desire to assist the customer and your expectation of future business.

8.2 Response to a Complaint over Damaged Merchandise

Situation Bergen's Furnishings has received a customer complaint regarding torn fabric on one piece of a recently purchased living room set. As a discount outlet, Bergen's attempts to make it clear to all customers prior to purchase that all sales are final. However, customers still complain when they find a problem once they get the merchandise home. And Bergen's must respond as diplomatically as possible.

The Letter Dear Mr. Hathaway:

Thank you for your letter of February 8. I am sorry to hear that the main sofa cushion of your Broyard Living Room Set is torn. While I appreciate that your set was just purchased and you are only asking to exchange that one piece of the set, I regret that we will not be able to comply.

You will notice on your bill of sale that all items purchased at Bergen's are purchased on a Final Sale basis only. To provide Bergen's customers with the best merchandise possible at the lowest prices, we ask prospective buyers to carefully inspect all pieces before the sale is completed. Signs are posted in every section of the store as a reminder that all sales are final. Our salespeople and cashiers also regularly remind customers of our Pre-Purchase Inspection and Final Sale policies.

In our 25 years of business, Bergen's Furnishings has earned a reputation for reliability, value, and customer service. And while we strive for customer satisfaction, we're sorry that we are unable to accept any returns or exchanges once merchandise has left Bergen's warehouse.

If I can help you in any other way, please don't hesitate to contact me. If you'd like, I can provide you with the names and phone numbers of two reliable furniture repair companies that do excellent work.

Sincerely,

General Manager

Key Points

- Acknowledge the customer's problem and express your regrets.
- Let the customer know if you are able to do what has been requested. If no particular resolution has been requested, ask what the customer wants or offer possible options.
- If a solution has been suggested, state your company's position and why you must take that position.
- Mention some of your company's attributes to back up your willingness to resolve the complaint. Keep a friendly tone throughout your letter—even if you can't give customers what they want.
- End with a sincere offer of assistance.

8.3 Letters to Handle Complaints over Warranty Coverage

Situation Whenever you sell something under warranty, expect customers to have questions about the extent of the warranty's coverage. On The Road Bicycle Shop sold Tom Ansdam an expensive racing bike. Mr. Ansdam put almost 5000 miles on the bike in less than a year. He discovered that the tires had worn on the inside rim and thought the warranty would cover their replacement. He sent a letter of inquiry, and On The Road Bicycle Shop responds.

The Letter Dear ______:

Thank you for your letter of March 12 regarding the warranty coverage on your SpeedX 3000 bicycle.

The 12-month warranty on the bicycle covers replacement of any defective part, excluding damage due to normal wear and tear. Your problem with the tires is not covered. Normally, one would expect to replace the tires after 2500 miles. And since you exceeded this mileage, we must charge you for the replacements.

We are sorry that we can not agree to your request. But, because you are such a good customer, we'll give your bike a clean-up and lube free of charge when you come in for your new tires.

Sincerely,

Store Manager

P.S.: We're glad to hear that you're using your bike so much. You must be really enjoying it.

Key Points

- Thank the customer for the inquiry.
- Explain the terms of the warranty.
- Express your regrets that the item is not covered.
- Offer some token or service to show the customer that, although you cannot grant the request, the customer is important and special to you.
- Add a personal note to maintain a positive bond with the customer.

8.4 Response to a Complaint over a Misunderstood Order Specification

Situation Precise Packaging Company has received a customer complaint regarding an incorrect order. In checking, PPC discovers that the mistake is the customer's fault. A letter must be written by the Customer Service Manager explaining this. While the resolution is easy (the incorrect items are stock sizes), this might not always be the case. When providing a product or service to custom specifications, very carefully check all specifications to avoid problems.

The Letter Dear ______:

As soon as I got off the phone with you this morning, I checked the paperwork on file for your June 1 order. According to what you told me, the three items shipped to you from our mailing tube line do not match the dimensions ordered.

By checking your original order and our confirmation, I believe I see how the problem occurred. I've enclosed copies of both documents.

As you can see, the order form was filled out in your office by hand. For each incorrect item shipped, the item you actually wanted was on the line right below. I think that whoever filled out the order form mistakenly wrote on the incorrect lines.

Our order confirmation lists the items shipped by product number only. Since the tube specifications are not included on this document, the mistake was not picked up by your office prior to shipment.

We are able to accept a return on the three items in question since they are stock sizes. Please send in a replacement order—typewritten only—and our driver will pick up the original order when the new one is delivered next week.

We're glad we could resolve this to your satisfaction. As always, we're happy to meet all your packaging needs.

Sincerely,

Customer Service Manager

Key Points

- Show your concern for the customer by prompt attention to the complaint.
- Restate the problem.
- Share the results of your investigation. Send back-up documentation if possible.
- Your main concern is to satisfactorily respond to the complaint. It is unnecessary to stress that the problem is the customer's fault.
- Tell the customer what you plan to do and when.
- Be sincere and courteous, even if the customer's demands cannot be met.
- Close with an expression of how much you value your customer and look forward to future business.

8.5 Response to a Complaint over a Customer's Treatment by an Employee

Situation A customer of Legs and More hosiery and lingerie shop feels mistreated by a salesperson and writes a letter of complaint. According to the customer, a salesperson attended to several other customers first, despite her being first on line. In investigating further, the store owner finds that the salesperson handled the situation appropriately but should have communicated her reasons to the customer at that time. But now, after a letter of complaint, an irate customer must be soothed.

The Letter Dear Mrs. Avent:

I can certainly understand your distress about the treatment you feel you received at our Legs and More store. Please accept our apologies for your displeasure and for any inconvenience it may have caused you.

Of course, I spoke to our salesperson, Ms. Green, to find out more about what happened. According to her, you asked her to check our stockroom for three pantyhose styles in sizes not available on the floor. The two other customers you refer to were at the register with merchandise and cash in hand, ready to pay. It appears that the problem was due to the fact that Ms. Green chose to ring up their sales first, then go to the basement to look for the items you requested.

Her thinking was to take an extra few minutes to complete the transactions she knew would be quick. She would have then been fully able to concentrate on your request, which she knew might take a while to satisfy. She certainly did not mean to offend or trouble you in any way, and offers you her sincerest apologies.

We're very glad you brought this situation to our attention. As a result, we're looking into new ways to best service and satisfy our customers. Again, we hope our apologies are accepted. Your business is very important to us, and we hope to see you at Legs and More again soon.

Sincerely,

Owner

Key Points

- Acknowledge the customer's feelings and offer your apologies for any inconvenience.
- Show that you take customers' complaints seriously but let them know you are also looking into it further.
- Thank customers for their complaints. Use what might have been viewed as a negative or unpleasant situation to improve your existing relationship.
- Let customers know how important their business is to you. Express your anticipation of a continued relationship.

8.6 Response to a Complaint over the Promptness of Problem Handling

Situation 800-Style, a mail order wallpaper company, has received a complaint that they have been excessively slow in handling the customer's problems. Because 800-Style's policy is to keep accurate records of all customer contacts, they are better able to respond to this kind of situation.

The Letter Dear Mrs. Lowinger:

Now that you've selected wallpaper for your home, I know how eager you are to receive it and get it hung. And I wish that 800-Style manufactured, stocked, and shipped orders as quickly as we receive them.

But, as our customer representative told you when you placed your order, 800-Style's unique service is to make thousands of wallpaper styles available to customers like yourself at 40 to 50 percent off the list price available at retail stores. All orders are custom-made by the manufacturer to give you the price advantage and benefit of door-to-door shipping.

Orders can take anywhere from 15 business days up to 8 weeks for delivery. If more than 8 weeks are required, the manufacturer will send you a card indicating the problem and the resolution you can expect.

Our records show six phone calls from you requesting more specific delivery information about your order. We truly wish we could provide that, but the 8-week period is not up yet and no production problems have been indicated by the manufacturer.

As a new 800-Style customer, you are undoubtedly anxious to receive your wallpaper. If you do not have it by July 15, let us know and we'll prepare a tracer right away.

We want you to be a satisfied customer! Since the majority of orders we handle are delivered within the promised 8 weeks, please try to be patient for the remainder of this period.

Sincerely,

Customer Service Manager

Key Points

- Since a slow response to customer needs indicates a lack of concern, tell the customer you care!
- Show that you empathize with what the customer is going through.
- If you keep careful records, let the customer know that you're aware of all contacts—when they took place and generally what was said.
- Restate whatever is causing the delay in customer satisfaction.
- Share any time frame for results that you have.
- Express concern. Make sure the customer knows you are taking every step possible to promptly resolve the matter.

8.7 Response to a Customer Threat of Legal Action

Situation Magic Incorporated sold a levitation device to The Amazing Jacoby. Jacoby performed the magic trick for the first time in front of an audience, and his volunteer fell to the ground instead of rising to the ceiling. Jacoby suffered embarrassment and has complained to the company, threatening to sue for damages. Magic Incorporated responds to Jacoby explaining their position that the manufacturer is not at fault.

The Letter Dear Mr. Jacoby:

We received your March 3 letter and are terribly sorry to hear of your displeasure with our Model #44, The Super Levitator.

We have investigated the alleged malfunction and find that the problem was not in the release mechanism as you suggested but in your misinterpretation of the instructional procedures. In every test we performed on the product, it worked perfectly. In fact, there are over 200 such units in use today without a single replication of your difficulty.

It appears to us that you pushed the release gear into level three instead of leaving it in an open position as instructed. You'll note on page 4 of your instruction booklet that we emphasize the importance of this step and make recommendations to ensure its correct application.

Of course, we can appreciate your disappointment at the failure of this illusion. While we believe we have made every effort to furnish you with an easy-to-use product and train you in its use, we understand that the procedures can be misunderstood.

Magic Incorporated is confident that we have not been negligent in this matter. However, we would like to extend the following to you: either a free personal training session with a Magic representative to instruct you in its use, or the return of your Model #44 for a refund of the original purchase price.

We've been doing business together for over six years now and want to keep you happy. Please let us know how we can satisfactorily resolve this matter.

Sincerely,

President

Key Points

- Acknowledge customers' complaints. You can express your regrets for their displeasure without accepting responsibility for the problem.
- Detail the facts as you see them. Show that you are taking this complaint seriously. By indicating your understanding of the customer's position, you're expressing your company's concern.
- Firmly state that you feel the complaint is unjustified, and explain your reasons for this conclusion.
- Offer options to resolve the matter. Remind persons with complaints of their "customer" status and of your history together.
- Close with a sincere expression of your hopes for a private resolution of the matter.

8.8 Response to a Complaint over Pricing Policies

Situation Mova Industries has announced a price increase for all orders received after December 1. In late November, the McDowell Financial Services Purchasing Agent tells Mova that she expects to place an order by the end of the month and is given a price quote. But the actual purchase order is not received in the Mova office until December 16. Mova contacts the customer to explain that the order cannot be accepted at the old price. McDowell complains about this decision, and Mova Industries must carefully respond to their customer.

The Letter Dear Lenore:

I regret that Mova Industries is unable to fill your recent purchase order as received. You're a valued customer, and Mova has always made every effort to meet your product and pricing needs. Of course, your continued business means a great deal to us.

I hope you can understand that, because of our stock limitations, I was only able to accept orders at the old prices if they were in our offices by December 1. Due to a cost increase in labor and raw materials, our new line will be priced at 5 to 10 percent higher than last year.

While I did quote a price to you on November 21, you did not give me a firm order or quantity to be reserved. Since your order was not received here until December 16, it can be filled only at the new pricing.

If you give us the go-ahead, delivery can be made by January 21. Please let me know how to proceed.

Sincerely,

John Willings
Sales Manager

Key Points

- Be straightforward with your customer about what you can or cannot do.
- Tell customers how much you value them. Express your hope that the problem will not prevent further business, even if you're unable to meet their request.
- Briefly explain the policy under discussion.
- State what you are able to do and when.
- Close with a reminder of the existing relationship and your hope for its continuation.

8.9 Response to a Complaint over Staffing Policy

Situation Al's Auto Exchange received a complaint from a customer who had to wait for 45 minutes before receiving service. A letter is sent to the customer.

The Letter Dear ______:

We have received your letter regarding our service department, and are sorry to hear that you had to wait over 45 minutes to be served.

Al's Auto Exchange has worked hard to create a customer-friendly service department. When we receive a complaint from an important customer like you, we immediately look for the cause of the problem and a solution that will help us serve you better.

You brought your car into the service department during our extended evening hours—at 7:30 P.M. We had two service managers working that night, and usually they can easily handle the workflow. Unfortunately, for some reason, three times the usual number of cars came in that night. There was no way that we could have anticipated this. In fact, this represented the most cars brought in for service in one evening in our 12 years of business.

However, you did have to wait and this is not right. We've taken measures to ensure that this does not happen again.

Please accept our apology for the inconvenience.

Sincerely,

Service Department Manager

P.S.: To make sure we're still friends, next time you need an oil change, it's on us!

Key Points

- Acknowledge the customer's complaint.
- State your commitment to excellent customer service.
- Explain the reason in a way that puts your company in the most positive light.
- Even though you were not wrong, apologize for the customer's inconvenience.
- Offer a small token to show the customer that you care.

9

Problem-Solving Letters

In the normal course of business, differences arise between company and customer. How these disputes are handled says a lot about the company and its commitment to customer service excellence.

The need for a problem-solving letter implies that the customer feels something should be handled one way while the company has taken a contrary position. It is up to the supplier or service company to make a choice. Do you compromise and try to find a resolution that tries to satisfy both parties, or do you maintain your position and hope the customer will accept it? Obviously, when the customer asks for something unreasonable, you have to stand firm.

A letter sent to resolve a problem should get to the point immediately. The situation should be described in simple, objective language, without comment or emotional coloring. If you feel you cannot accommodate the customer's request, explain why as briefly as possible in a logical manner. Always appeal to the customer's sense of fair play. Often a good strategy is to ask customers to "stand in your shoes" to see how they would handle the dispute.

The cardinal rule for handling customer problems is to be consistent in your actions. Company policies should dictate your decisions—with some flexibility built in. The worst thing to do is to treat different customers with similar problems differently. Not only do you expose yourself to the threat of legal problems, but you are likely to lose your ability to act with conviction and integrity.

The bottom line is that disputes with customers are always difficult to handle. Your decision and actions may make the difference between a lost customer and a satisfied one.

Key Points

- As long as you are in business, expect to have problems with customers. No matter how you handle things, some will be dissatisfied. But, by maintaining a consistent, commonsense approach, you can earn most customers' respect and loyalty.
- Problem-solving letters should be concise, to-the-point, and unemotional. Objectively describe the situation, and present your resolution in a straightforward way.
- Be fair, consistent, and flexible.

9.1 Letter to Solve a Price Dispute

Situation Jim Smith ordered the *Handyman's Home Library* from Echo Publishing at a promotional price for the entire set. He has decided to keep six of the volumes and return two, which he is entitled to do. The dispute arose because Mr. Smith expects to be refunded at the per-volume price for the two books rather than at the prorated promotional price. The difference between the two prices is significant. Echo Publishing wishes to keep Mr. Smith as a customer. But they also want him to keep the six books he's already paid for and accept what the publisher considers to be the proper refund.

The Letter Dear Mr. Smith:

I am writing you to resolve the situation that has been brought to my attention regarding a refund for two volumes of the Handyman's Library you purchased on July 20.

According to your customer records, the set was purchased at a special discount price of $189 instead of the regular per-volume price of $280.

While we are very pleased that you think highly of the six volumes you've chosen to keep, the discounted price is only available to buyers of the complete Handyman's Library. Your decision to return two of these volumes is fine, and we are happy to issue you a refund. However, your refund will be based on the set price of $23.62 per volume rather than the $35.00 single volume price.

I'm sure you understand that we cannot refund more money for these items than you actually paid. However, because we do want you to be a satisfied customer, I have enclosed a $10 discount certificate that can be used when ordering any new Echo publications. Our *Home Building Encyclopedia,* due out this spring, is one that might be of interest to you. I've added your name to our list of customers to receive all new product catalogs.

I'm sure that you appreciate our position. We hope that this solution is acceptable to you and that we can continue to be of future service.

Sincerely,

Billing Manager

Key Points

- It is sometimes helpful to have a new person enter the dispute saying that they have been called in for a final solution.
- Briefly restate the situation.
- State how your company plans to resolve the dispute. You may need to explain why this decision was made but do it as simply and briefly as possible.
- Express your desire for the customer to be satisfied, even if you are not resolving the problem in the way requested. If possible, offer customers something extra to compensate for having to turn them down.
- Close by sharing your expectation of future business.

9.2 Letter to Solve a Late Delivery Problem

Situation Riteway manufactures canned food products sold through food distributors to supermarkets state-wide. Their last three orders to Norgate Distributors have been late, and Norgate has asked for compensation. Upon checking, Riteway finds that one late delivery was unavoidable due to a major storm and the other two were not actually their fault. Riteway drivers had contacted Norgate to make delivery appointments and would have been on schedule. However, because all loading docks at Norgate were full, the drivers were told to call back to reschedule. When the drivers called back, the rescheduled dates were later than the companies had originally arranged. Riteway's Director of Operations writes the following letter to the customer.

The Letter Dear Jim:

I understand your concern that Riteway deliver on schedule. Of course, it is imperative that Norgate be able to deliver to its supermarket locations on time so that out-of-stock situations do not occur. Upon review, there seems to be an easy solution to the problem.

Riteway drivers always phone Norgate's loading dock the morning of the day they expect to arrive. In two of the three cases in question, by the time they called, all loading docks were already reserved for that day. Since our drivers are instructed not to wait overnight in order to make a delivery, by the time they returned to your area, the deliveries were late.

I've now instructed our Order Clerks to arrange delivery appointments with Norgate one week prior to delivery. Drivers will call the loading dock only if an unforeseen problem requires a change in the appointment.

Of course, we are very sorry that this situation caused you difficulty and expect our policy change to eliminate any future problem. To compensate you for the inconvenience, Riteway would like to extend your "Jump Into Spring" discount schedule until May 15. This means an extra six weeks of savings for any Riteway orders placed during the extension period.

I certainly hope Norgate is satisfied with this resolution. Please let me know if I can be of any further help.

Sincerely,

Harvey Linder
Director of Operations

Key Points

- State why you are writing. Let the customer know you are aware of the specifics of the problem.
- Offer a solution to the problem. Be concise.
- Express your regrets for any inconvenience they have experienced. If possible, propose some sort of compensation—a discount, gift, refund, or extra service.

9.3 Letter to Solve a Problem Involving Customer Treatment

Situation One of Computer Specialties' customers has complained to its sales representative that the Service Department manager treated him rudely and unfairly. The sales rep realizes that this problem has gotten out-of-hand and asks the general manager to resolve the dispute. A letter is sent to the customer.

The Letter Dear ______:

Jim Anderson has informed me of the problem you are having with the manager of our Service Department.

As I understand the situation, your model W-2000 Laser Printer is not feeding correctly. You brought the printer to our Service Department on September 21 for repair under warranty. The printer was fixed and returned to you. On October 15, you brought the printer back for a similar malfunction. Because your warranty had by then expired, you were charged for the repair. You feel that you should not be charged because the original problem was never completely fixed. Our service department says that the printer was repaired, a new feeding mechanism was installed, and that the new problem is not related to the original one.

In addition, Jim tells me that you believe that the sales manager was rude to you and offered no explanation for the repair charges.

First, let me assure you that we would not charge you for a repair that was incorrectly executed under warranty. We have built our business—and reputation—on our repair service. We've even won awards as the best in the Southwest for three consecutive years.

I've spoken with Jane Bilkson, our Service Department manager, and have reviewed the paperwork for the September 21 and October 15 repairs. While both problems resulted in feeding jams, they were caused by the malfunction of different parts. On each occasion, a different part was replaced. Therefore, your second repair had nothing to do with the first.

Jane and I also discussed the manner in which you were treated. Jane will be calling you to apologize for the lack of communication, which appears to be the root of the problem. I am sure you will be treated in the manner you expect in the future.

I understand how frustrating it is to have a similar problem after having a repair made. While you are responsible for the charges incurred for the second repair, I want to do something to try to make up for the unsatisfactory treatment you feel you received. I've enclosed a $75 voucher, redeemable in supplies and/or future repair work. Please accept this as a token of our apology.

If you'd like to discuss this situation further, please call me at 555-5555.

Sincerely,

Everett Ellington
General Manager

Key Points

- Describe the situation as you understand it. Be as objective as possible. Do not offer opinions.
- Explain to the customer why you believe you were justified in acting as you did.
- When you were wrong, say so. Apologize for your mistake or inappropriate actions.
- Show that the customer's satisfaction is important by offering something extra to demonstrate your desire to resolve the problem in an equitable manner.
- In closing, make yourself available for additional discussion if the customer wants it.

9.4 Letter to Solve a Dispute Over the Terms of an Agreement or Contract

Situation Jefferson Bakery has a yearly service contract with Stillwell Exterminators. Upon receiving their January statement, Jefferson Bakery refuses to pay for additional charges billed since they believe their service contract covers these additional services. Stillwell writes to Jefferson, explaining the terms of the contract and how they believe the dispute should be resolved.

The Letter Dear ______:

I'm writing in reference to your inquiry about service contract, number AS1287-4532.

In your letter of January 9, you dispute the charge on invoice 00234 for pest control services. While your contract for this calendar year includes bimonthly service, the additional charge is for supplemental service that you requested to help prepare for the state inspection.

If you refer to paragraph 6 of your service contract, additional service visits are to be billed at $100 per hour. The November 23 service call lasted 2½ hours; therefore a charge of $250 was added to your monthly statement.

If the terms of our contract were not fully explained to you, we apologize. You are an important customer to us, and we certainly do not want to jeopardize our relationship.

I hope this clarifies the disputed charge. As you can see, we charged you only for extra service performed at your request.

We do have other service agreement options that would include additional service calls. You may enjoy some savings in changing your agreement in the future. I'd be happy to discuss this with you at your convenience.

Sincerely,

Service Manager

Key Points

- Let the customer know why you are writing.
- Refer to the portions of your contract that have determined your handling of the dispute. You may actually want to quote or reprint all relevant parts.
- Make sure to tell your customers how important they are to you and that you are only attempting to resolve the matter in a way that meets the terms of your agreement.
- You can close by offering to meet with the customer to review the agreement, and possibly to change or adapt the specifics to meet any new customer needs or requirements.

10

Letters Explaining Errors

Customers are often of a mixed mind about errors made by the companies they choose to do business with. Usually, a customer's concerns are that the product or service is promptly and accurately provided and that their payment is correctly processed.

If either of these steps is handled incorrectly, then the prime concern is that adjustments are made with a minimum of inconvenience and a maximum of concern. To a large degree, customers don't care why the error occurred. So "complaining" to a customer or acting as if any reason justifies an error is always a mistake.

However, as long as your explanation is not presented or perceived as a rationalization, and as long as it is kept as brief as possible, you may want to explain the causes. It is most important to remember not to present this explanation as if it justifies the error.

Key Points

- Regardless of the specifics, customers care most about your rectifying the error, not why it happened.
- The last thing a customer wants is an explanation that conveys the attitude that it justifies the mistake.
- Even though some situations are out of your control, customers do not want to hear your complaints about your staff who are out sick or the computer glitch you discovered.
- If you do choose to explain an error, keep it short and simple.

10.1 Letter Explaining an Order Content Error

Situation Pierre D'Autumn Art School has purchased a large range of canvases from Everything for Artists for their fall session. When the order arrives, the purchasing agent finds that they have been shorted on the canvas size most often used. They have received only 12 of the 12 dozen ordered. Everything for Artists responds to their customer with the following letter.

The Letter Dear Jean:

I appreciate how concerned you are that your fall semester starts next Tuesday and you received only one dozen 16 × 20 basic white canvases from us. As soon as you called me, I shipped you an additional four dozen 16 × 20 midline whites, which should cover your needs for at least the first three weeks of classes. While these are regularly priced at an additional $4 each, you'll only be billed for the basic quality price. These should be delivered by Friday, in plenty of time for you to set up for classes.

I'm terribly sorry that your order was not shipped as requested—and that I was unaware of this until you contacted me. Upon checking, I found that we had an unexpected stock shortage of your 16 × 20s. Our shipping department didn't realize how important that particular item is to you and assumed a back order, with shipment by September 21, would be satisfactory. I've now made sure they know about your particular needs, and no substitutions or back orders will be made without contacting both of us first.

Since new stock of the 16 × 20 basics are expected by the 10th, the balance of your order for that item will be shipped then.

Your satisfaction is very important to us. Please let me know right away if the arrangements I've made will work for you. If not, I'll be happy to make any adjustments I can.

Sincerely,

Customer Service Manager

Key Points

- Express your concern about the mistake. Tell the customer what has been done to rectify it. Reassure the customer that your actions will eliminate any anticipated inconvenience.
- Briefly explain the cause of the error and what you have done to make sure it does not happen again.
- Let customers know how important they are to you and that you're willing to do whatever is necessary to satisfy them.

10.2 Letter Explaining a Delivery Error

Situation When Rainbow Paints attempts to deliver an order to Chez Moi Decorating, the driver finds that the store is closed for remodeling. Upon further checking, they find that Chez Moi's order had given specific instructions for delivery to a substitute address during the remodeling period. A letter of explanation must now be written to the customer.

The Letter Dear ______:

Please excuse us. When our driver returned from attempting to make your paint delivery, we found that you had indeed notified us of your plans to close for remodeling during the week of August 15.

We regret that this information, plus the substitute delivery address you gave us, were not passed along to the scheduler who sets up all Rainbow's delivery routes. Jan, the individual you usually work with in our Order Department, was out sick when this scheduling took place. Her absence probably contributed to our making this error. We have already instituted a new checking system to make sure a mistake of this kind cannot happen again.

I understand that a new delivery date has already been set up for next week, but I wanted to personally apologize to you for the inconvenience. As a long-time customer, your satisfaction is always important to us.

Sincerely,

President

Key Points

- Apologize for your error and confirm that you had been given the correct information.
- Offer a brief explanation for the mistake. Show that correcting the mistake is very important to you by stating what you've done to ensure that it does not happen again.
- Remind customers of your long-standing relationship and how important they are to you.

10.3 Letter Explaining a Pricing Error

Situation Island Counseling Center orders regularly from the Children's Mental Health Foundation—brochures, fact sheets, videos, and other educational items—to distribute to the families and individuals who use their facilities. Island has purchased a revolving rack of information pieces from CMHF and has been billed $1,750. Later that month, when the Center receives CMHF's new catalog, they see that the printed price for the information rack is really $750 and that they have been overcharged. When the Foundation is told of the error, they must respond to their customer.

The Letter Dear Dr. Longstreet:

While I've been told that our Billing Department has already sent you an adjusted invoice for your complete Children's Mental Health Foundation Information Rack, please accept my personal apology for our error. Island Counseling Center is a valued customer and one we've supplied since our inception seven years ago.

Of course, we hate to make an error of any kind, and we hope this one did not cause any undue difficulties. It appears that the mistake was due to human error, and we've already instituted additional training time and cross-checks for our staff to avoid problems like this in the future.

We've had a very positive response so far to the rack you purchased. Please let us know how your staff and clients react to the new publications. Your satisfaction is very important to us.

Sincerely,

Chairman

Key Points

- Apologize for your company's error, and tell the customer what is being done to correct it.
- Let customers know how important they are to you and how upset you are that the error occurred.
- State briefly why the error occurred and what has been done to prevent it from happening again.
- You may want to shift the focus to the item purchased and mention something positive about it.
- Close by reiterating how important your customer's satisfaction is to you.

10.4 Letter Explaining an Error Caused by an Employee Mistake

Situation Smith & Weston has reordered stationery from a commercial printer who produces all their promotional materials. Because of their existing relationship, the order is placed informally, over the phone. But when it comes time for the work to be delivered, Smith & Weston discovers that John's Print Shop has printed 5,000 envelopes instead of 5,000 sheets of letterhead. Although the correct order is now in production, John writes his customer the following letter.

The Letter Dear Bob:

Even though your correct order—5,000 sheets of letterhead—has already been rescheduled as a SUPER RUSH, I wanted to again apologize for our error.

We've taken orders over the phone before and never had a problem like this. The day we took your order, we were short staffed, and someone from another department was filling in to help out. We've already instituted new policies to prevent this type of mistake from happening again. Also, in the future, I'd appreciate your following up any order placed over the phone with a written confirmation.

Your stationery will be delivered this Friday. I've taken the liberty of printing an additional 1,000 sheets at no charge as a more tangible apology for any inconvenience we've caused you. I'll also hold the envelopes in case you need them in the future.

Sincerely,

John Minton
President

Key Points

- Tell your customer how the error has been remedied.
- Apologize (again) for your company's mistake and briefly explain how it happened. Even if it was an individual's fault, there's no need to name names in your explanation.
- Let yours customers know that you've instituted new policies to prevent any future errors. If appropriate, ask them to handle similar situations differently too.
- You may want to offer something extra as an apology. If not, you'd want to make sure customers know how important they are to you.

10.5 Letter Explaining an Error Caused by a Customer Mistake

Situation KoolAire Repair Service has an appointment scheduled on May 21 with Buffet Industries. When the KoolAire representative shows up, he finds Buffet is closed for the day due to inventory, and he is unable to gain entry to the equipment rooms to work. That same day, KoolAire's Service Manager writes a letter to Roger Bond, the Buffet manager who had made the service appointment.

The Letter Dear Roger:

I'm sure you know by now that our KoolAire agent was at Buffet Industries earlier today for your service appointment. Unfortunately, due to your inventory schedule, he was unable to gain entrance to do his job.

When we set up this appointment, I recall how important it was for you to have the servicing done prior to the Memorial Day weekend. And we did whatever we could to fit this appointment in at a time and day that was convenient for you.

Unfortunately, our service schedule is entirely booked for the next five weeks—until early July. I know this is well past the date when you needed attention, but because of your unavailability, the earliest date we could reschedule is July 9, 9 A.M.

I understand that this might be inconvenient for you and have made note that you will get the first cancellation if one occurs prior to that date. For now, please call me as soon as you receive this to confirm July 9.

Sincerely,

Service Manager

Key Points

- Present the situation in a concise and objective manner.
- Without any emotional coloring or assigning blame, you can let the customer know that you fulfilled your responsibilities.
- Let the customer know specifically how you will be able to resolve the situation.
- Show that you are still willing to do your best to accommodate the customer but that, since the error was his, you may not be able to meet the original requirements.

10.6 Letter Explaining an Error Caused by a Difference in Taste

Situation It is Nassau Marketing Consultants' policy to have all clients give final approval to any promotional pieces to be printed. To avoid postproduction complaints, the client must sign off on all work as a last check prior to printing. When Jan Swift & Associates complains about the colors of their new brochure, the president of Nassau Marketing responds with this letter.

The Letter Dear Jan:

As I told you on the phone, I did see the finished pieces for your new brochure before they were shipped to you and found nothing out of order. In response to your request, though, I reviewed your client folder to check the records on your brochure's development.

Our Bob Nelson worked on this with Madge Evans from your office. In keeping with our standard policy, every step of the brochure's development is on file with Madge's signature. I am sorry that you are not satisfied with the look of your brochure, but our contract to initiate the work states that Madge would be acting as your firm's representative for this job. Color swatches were sent to Madge for approval and, as you can see on the enclosed, her selections were the ones used.

After I heard from you, I also showed your brochure to Jim Williams and Sara Owens. I know you've worked with them before, and I seem to remember that you always felt they had excellent design taste. While your opinion is really the only one that counts, both Jim and Sara felt the piece turned out very well and should get the kind of customer reaction you're hoping for.

If you still feel dissatisfied with the colors when you're ready to reprint, you can select any others you'd prefer. Bob Nelson will still be the account executive of record, but I'd like to be part of any further job actions for Jan Swift & Associates. Let me know if you'd also like to be involved when the time comes.

We want you to be happy with the work we've done for you, and I believe you have been over the years. Let's give this brochure a chance to do its job and then see what the results are.

Sincerely,

President

Key Points

- Make sure the customer knows you are doing whatever is necessary to investigate the mistake.
- Explain briefly and honestly how the problem occurred, as long as you are absolutely sure of your facts and have records to back them up.
- Put the focus back on resolving the customer's problem as quickly as possible.

10.7 Letter Explaining a Discount Error

Situation Brager Technical Services purchases three-ring notebooks from E-Z Present for their looseleaf product. During a price promotion, Brager placed a large order to be delivered in five shipments over an eight-month period. Brager's invoice for the final order does not reflect the discounted price they had been promised. E-Z Presents must respond to Brager and explain the error.

The Letter

Dear Mr. Kronwith:

We've corrected the error you pointed out in our October bill. As you will see on the enclosed invoice, the total due now reflects the 20 percent discount offered in our Spring Price Promotion. According to E-Z Presents' records, this is your final order at this special pricing.

Please pardon the oversight. Since the promotion required all shipments to be made by August 30, our Billing Department was unaware that you had special approval for a September delivery as part of your March 15 PO.

Thank you for your understanding. E-Z Presents appreciates your business and looks forward to supplying you in the future.

Sincerely,

Customer Service Manager

Key Points

- Show the customer that your error has been corrected. Describe the customer's current status.
- Apologize for your error and briefly explain why it happened.
- Tell customers that you appreciate their patience and refer to your anticipation of future business.

10.8 Letter Explaining a Tax-Charged Error

Situation McCullough Collins Publishers has received a complaint from Baird County Psychiatric Society of a $138.29 overcharge on their most recent order. When McCullough Collins uncovers the reason for the error, they must contact their customer to explain what happened and show that the mistake has been corrected.

The Letter Dear Dr. Pawling:

Enclosed is an adjusted bill for your May 13 order for 500 copies of *A New Look at Today's Adolescents.* We have removed the $138.29 in taxes that you were charged in error.

Of course, as soon as we looked at your original order and correspondence, we found the copy of your tax-exempt form. Please accept our apologies for overlooking this.

Our records have now been adjusted to show this change and the fact that you are not to be taxed on any future orders. Thank you for your patience. We look forward to serving you in the future.

Sincerely,

Accounts Manager

Key Points

- Let the customer know right away that you have corrected the error.
- Briefly explain where the error was found and why it occurred.
- Reassure customers that it will not happen again. You may also want to extend your thanks for their patience.
- Express your expectation of future business.

11

Reactivating an Inactive Customer

Companies work very hard to develop relationships with their customers. Yet even the most progressive, well conceived, and best executed customer care program loses a certain percentage of customers every year.

These once satisfied, once active customers are like Sleeping Beauties—lost in suspended animation and awaiting new life. Most companies spend a large percentage of their promotional budget acquiring new customers, while too often completely ignoring inactive customers. Marketers forget the fundamental tenet that, "It's easier to activate an old customer than acquire a new one."

Letters sent to activate past customers should follow specific guidelines. An important consideration is the recency of the letter with respect to the last purchase. Companies need up-to-date information about their customers, their purchasing habits, and their date of last purchase. Once a customer passes the "two times" missed normal purchasing cycle, reactivation becomes more difficult.

The reactivation letter can announce anything new about the supplier that the customer may find of interest. New equipment, improvements, products, and the like are all newsworthy and may provide a reason for customers to renew their relationship with the supplier.

The reactivation letter must include three elements:

1. It must begin in an attention-getting manner that makes the customer take notice. A letter that is not read is never acted on.

2. It must reinforce the past positive relationship between the company and customer. Always remind the customer of previous transactions, accommodations, and service. When possible, use personal references and anecdotes to reestablish rapport.

3. It must make a special offer that entices the customer to take action. Discounts, free merchandise, premiums, and so on are effective motivators.

Key Points

- Inactive customers represent a lucrative profit center.
- Don't allow too much time to pass before sending the reactivation letter.
- To stay on top of inactive customers, adequate management information systems must be in place.
- Letters sent to inactive customers must grab their attention, reinforce the past relationship, and offer an incentive for the customer to buy again.

11.1 Letter to Customer Who Hasn't Ordered Recently

Situation In reviewing accounts, a sales manager discovers that a good customer, who had been making purchases on a monthly schedule for years, has not purchased anything in six months. A letter is sent to the customer to learn the reason for this lack of activity and to promise to resolve any difficulties so that the customer can resume buying.

The Letter Dear ______:

I received a computer printout this morning and couldn't believe my eyes . . .

It showed that the last time you ordered from us was over six months ago. When I checked your buying history, I found that Acme Marine has been an excellent customer for many years.

May I ask you what happened? It is very unusual for us to lose a customer without knowing about a specific problem or situation.

Please tell us if we did something wrong. We work very hard to find and keep good customers like you. And we are prepared to go the extra mile to solve any problem you may have experienced.

Would you please jot down your thoughts in the space provided below and return this letter to me in the SASE? Your remarks will be greatly appreciated.

Your Comments Here Please

____

____

____

Thank you for your time. We will do everything we can to rectify any problems you have had with us. We look forward to working with Acme Marine again.

Sincerely,

Sales Manager

Key Points

- Use an attention-getting opening to involve the customer.
- Briefly state your concern.
- Tell the customer how important his or her business is to your company.
- Ask the customer to relate the reason for the lack of business.
- State your intention to "go the extra mile" to fulfill the customer's needs.

11.2 Letter to a Customer Who Hasn't Ordered in Over One Year

Situation When a customer hasn't ordered for over a year, it's a serious problem. Action must be taken immediately to discover the problem and reactivate the customer. This letter is designed to ascertain the problem and motivate the customer to buy again.

The Letter

The Answer Is: Over One Year Ago

What's the Question?

Dear ______:

The question is, "When did we receive our last order from Aarcom International?"

It's true! It's been over a year since you placed an order with us and we're very concerned.

Over the past five years, Aarcom has been one of our better customers. In fact, because of your consistent business, we offered you many services unavailable to other customers. Among these were in-house warehousing and staggered billing.

Why does an excellent customer stop ordering? There can only be three reasons:

1. You no longer use our product.
2. You found a better supplier.
3. We did something terribly wrong.

We know that number one is not true. You still use wire screening. As for the second reason, we doubt it. Our reputation and leadership position speak for themselves. Number three worries us. We're not aware of any problem, but . . .

If we erred, please let us know. Then we can make up for any difficulties you have suffered.

And, to make it easier to get started with us again, we want to offer you a significant discount on your first reorder.

Please call for an immediate quotation and for your special pricing. You'll be glad you did!

Sincerely,

Sales Manager

Key Points

- An attention-getting question peaks the customer's interest.
- The company's concerns are expressed and the past relationship described and reinforced.
- A special offer is used to motivate the customer to reopen communications with the supplier.

11.3 Letter Offering a Special Gift for Activating an Account

Situation Jeffrey Office Supply has lost many customers to the new, superstores. To try to win back some of that business, customers who have not ordered within six months are sent a special promotion offering a gift.

The Letter

A Special Gift for a Special Customer

Dear ______:

We've reserved a copy of the *Business Executive's Desk Reference Set* just for you. It's a handy resource for busy executives that includes a dictionary, thesaurus, and unique encyclopedia of business terms, facts, and pointers. We know that you will find it a valuable tool you'll use everyday.

Why are we offering you this gift? Our reason is simple. It's been quite some time since you placed an order with us. And, since that time, we've expanded our line with dozens of new, exciting products. The gift is our way of asking you to take a second look at Jeffrey Office Supply. We know that, when you review our new catalog (sent to you along with your gift), you will find our products to be of exceptional value.

Of particular interest are the new ExcecuLife Chairs. This ergonomically designed desk and work seating system offers back, neck, and leg support not found in ordinary office furniture. In fact, studies have shown that ExecuLife actually reduces back strain by 40 percent.

To receive your FREE gift and our new, 84-page, full-color catalog, return the enclosed card or call 1-800-555-5555.

Sincerely,

Sales Manager

P.S.: The FREE *Business Executive's Desk Reference Set* was designed to take up only six square inches of desk space so that you can keep it in reach without cluttering your workspace.

Key Points

- Use the gift offer as a means of gaining customers' attention.
- Sell the gift by describing its benefits to customers.
- Take this opportunity to mention new products, special services, and other benefits that the customer may be interested in.
- Tell the reader exactly what to do next.

11.4 Letter Offering a Special Discount for Activating an Account

Situation Robbins Paints has decided to offer a discount to customers who have been inactive over the last year. A letter is sent to them.

The Letter Dear ______:

Because you are a Robbins Paints commercial customer in good standing, we'd like to make you a special offer. Until November 25, you can deduct an extra 20 percent off orders placed for paint or painting supplies.

As you know, Robbins Paints' prices are the lowest in the Springfield area. And we carry every major brand as well as our own Robbins Paints line.

So why not take advantage of this extraordinary discount! It's not available to the public—just to good commercial customers like you.

To make sure you receive the discount, use the special account number listed below:

Your Special Account # is A-1287

We look forward to seeing you soon.

Sincerely,

Sales Manager

P.S.: With the special 20-percent discount off our already low prices, you'll pay about half of what other paint suppliers are charging!

Key Points

- Let the customer know that he or she is a customer in good standing even though no purchases have been made during the past year.
- Announce your special discount and its terms.
- Explain to the customer the benefits of purchasing from you.

11.5 Invitation to Special Sale If an Account Is Activated

Situation Maxwell's has decided to open its store after hours to customers who have not ordered recently as a means of reestablishing a relationship with them. The after-hours gala will include a fashion show, special discounts, and other features. A letter is sent inviting past customers.

The Letter

You're Invited!!!

Dear ______:

We're holding a special, gala open house at Maxwell's for all our friends who haven't visited us lately. It's a great way to see the latest fashions, take advantage of special one-day sale prices, enjoy gourmet refreshments, and get reacquainted with Maxwell's.

At this special event, you'll . . .

- See all the new fashions before anyone else.
- Hear a fascinating talk on fashion and style given by a famous New York designer.
- Taste delicious hors d'oeuvres prepared by outstanding area chefs.
- And much, much more.

The gala will be held on Tuesday, September 11 at 8:00 P.M. To receive your FREE VIP ticket to this private party, RSVP today by calling 555-6789.

We look forward to seeing you again.

Sincerely,

Store Manager

P.S.: Dress is casual, but the fun will be intense. So mark your calendar now!

Key Points

- Get the customer's attention with a strong headline.
- Sell the special event by detailing all the enjoyable activities.
- Explain to the customer that he or she has been chosen to attend this exclusive sale.
- Provide specific instructions on what the customer should do next.
- Use the P.S. to reinforce the appeal of the invitation.

11.6 Information About a New Service

Situation Kelly Plastics, an injection molding manufacturer, has lost customers to competitors with better technology. A new CAD system has been purchased to offer needed technical support. A letter is sent announcing the new service to those inactive customers suspected of switching to other suppliers because of their technological advantage.

The Letter Dear ______:

Something exciting has happened at Kelly Plastics that can make your job a lot easier. The good news is that we've installed a new computer-aided design (CAD) system. It's the Pueblo 1100, the same state-of-the-art system used by NASA. The CAD system will let you and our team of designers quickly make corrections to your designs at the modeling stage and still meet your deadline. Ordinarily, minor redesigns might be neglected because of the lack of time. Now we can make those changes, in-house, in a matter of hours.

We'd like to invite you to a demonstration of the new CAD system so that you'll be familiar with all its capabilities. We've scheduled three demonstrations:

June 21 at 11:00
June 23 at 11:00
June 28 at 11:00

If you have the time, we will be serving lunch at 12:30. Please call to make a reservation as seating will be limited.

We know that the addition of the CAD system will enable us to serve you better. And we're offering six free hours of CAD with any new project booked in July, August, or September.

Call us today to take advantage of this new technology and for your free six hours of design.

General Manager

Key Points

- Announce the new service. Explain its advantages.
- Offer a demonstration, presentation, or tour.
- Make a special offer to entice the customer to respond.
- Tell the customer what action to take next.

11.7 Information About a New Product Line

Situation Pro-Golf Products is using a new product line to reactivate old customers. A letter describing the product and its profit-building advantages is sent to build interest in Pro-Golf.

The Letter Dear ______:

Over 1000 golf pro shops like yours have discovered that adding our new line of CARRY-LITE golf bags can mean big profits.

Yes! You can earn a hefty 60 percent profit when you order a dozen bags to sell in your pro shop.

Best of all, the CARRY-LITE bag sells itself. Since it was introduced six months ago, it has become the fastest selling golf bag in the business. It received rave reviews from Golfer Magazine and was voted "Best Bag" by *Golf Equipment News*.

When you place an initial stocking inventory of 12 bags, you receive a unique revolving display that tells the fascinating history of the golf bag. It really draws attention to our bags and is a unique addition to your pro shop's decor. In fact, many pro shops have ordered more than one display. It's destined to be a collectors' item.

Just return the enclosed order card, and we'll rush you a dozen CARRY-LITE golf bags in assorted colors along with your FREE display unit.

We know you'll find that, once you offer the CARRY-LITE, it will become one of your best selling items.

Sincerely,

Sales Manager

P.S.: Because it's been a long time since you last ordered, we'll take an additional 5 percent off if you call in your order today. It's our way of welcoming you back to Pro-Golf Products.

Key Points

- Open with a powerful statement that will motivate the customer to read further.
- Offer facts or statistics that reinforce your selling point.
- Suggest other reasons for buying.
- Make an attractive additional offer. Reinforce the customer status of the reader.

11.8 Letter to New Buyer at Inactive Account

Situation Often a change in personnel offers a special opportunity for a company to revitalize a waning relationship with an account. Roger-Klein Productions has learned that a new purchasing manager has been hired at Arlington Industries and jumps at the chance to regain this company's business.

The Letter Dear ______:

Congratulations on your appointment as purchasing agent. I'm sure you'll find your new position at Arlington Industries to be both challenging and rewarding.

As you may know, Roger-Klein Productions has provided training video production services for Arlington in the past although we have not done business recently. You may even have seen the video we did introducing your company to new employees when you were hired. I know Arlington has been successfully using that video for over three years.

Over the last six months, we have expanded our production capabilities with new equipment, additional staff, and a new facility. We are now prepared to handle any sales training, staff development, or management training project that you have.

Let's get together to discuss what we can offer you once you've had a chance to catch your breath. I'm sure you'll find Roger-Klein a valuable resource.

Sincerely,

General Manager

Key Points

- Extend your congratulations to the new appointee.
- Describe your past relationship in positive terms.
- Sell your capabilities.
- Ask for a meeting once the new manager has adjusted to the change.

11.9 Letter Explaining New Technology to an Inactive Account

Situation The American Health Club has installed state-of-the-art equipment that simulates training used by world class athletes. In a letter to inactive members, they announce this new equipment and offer a free session with trainers to entice old members back into the club.

The Letter

You Can Now Attain the Peak Conditioning of
A World Class Athlete!

Dear ______:

We're writing to past American Health Club members to announce a revolutionary new training program that actually simulates the physical and psychological challenges faced by the world class athlete.

Have you ever wondered how top athletes achieve their remarkable conditioning? The answer is simple. Physiologists and trainers of the athletic elite have recently discovered that a combination of muscle group development and resistance/endurance training creates capabilities beyond what seemed possible only a few short years ago.

Now this new methodology is available in the Pro Galaxy 5000 machine. And American Health Club is the first health/fitness facility in the Southwest to offer this new technology to its members.

To learn how you can benefit, call 555-4447 today! Set up a special demonstration appointment—and, if you bring along your workout clothes, you'll get a free trial workout with our special training staff.

Sincerely,

General Manager

Key Points

- Use an attention-getting headline.
- Pique the customer's interest by mentioning some strong benefits of the new technology and your company.
- Tell the customer specifically what you are offering and what to do next.

12
Goodwill Letters

Of course, you want to create as much goodwill as possible with your customers. And you can create it in many ways:

- By providing what you promised when you promised it.
- By being responsive to your customer's concerns, interests, and needs.
- By contributing in any way you can to your customer's success.
- By always remembering that what exists between you and your customer is not only a buyer-seller relationship but a relationship between two individuals. The goodwill you create by treating your customer well extends itself to all your business dealings.

In the course of any customer relationship, there are countless opportunities for strengthening the bond between you. Some, like the ones just listed, are mostly business-related, but others can be more personal.

If you remember that customers are people, you'll know that, just like you, they like to be remembered on special occasions, congratulated for their accomplishments, and acknowledged in times of difficulty. A personal note in any of these situations goes a long way to creating the kind of good feelings that encourage customer loyalty.

The tone of a personal note to a customer should always reflect the character of your relationship. If you and your customer are cordial to one another but rarely discuss matters outside the office, your correspondence should not be overly informal. However, if you have a more familiar side to your relationship, it's perfectly alright to let that show in these types of notes.

Key Points

- Goodwill letters are excellent opportunities to strengthen the bond between you and your customer.
- Remember that customers are individuals with personal needs and concerns. Acknowledging something special or new, offering congratulations or condolences, and just remembering a birthday are just a few ways you can create goodwill with a client.
- The tone of your letter should reflect the personality of your relationship as well as the reason you are writing.
- Take advantage of all opportunities to create goodwill with your customers. If you don't, your competitors will.

12.1 Congratulations on Business Expansion

Situation Eleanor and Martin Caswell have opened a list rental division to their existing marketing services company. A graphic design firm they regularly use writes to congratulate them on this expansion of their business.

The Letter Dear Eleanor and Martin:

Congratulations on Information Distribution's new List Services Division! I was so pleased to hear of this important addition to your company. I'm sure you'll turn it into as much of a success as your publishing and information services group.

I've already mentioned your expansion to one or two associates who occasionally need list information and rentals. Let me know if I can be of assistance in any other ways to your new endeavor.

Best of luck,

Steven Borman

Key Points

- Congratulate your customers on the expansion of their business.
- Compliment their success, their good timing, or whatever you feel contributed to this growth.
- Offer your support and assistance in your customer's continued growth.

12.2 Congratulations on New Offices

Situation Balthos Industries is a long-time customer of Gardner Harrington. When Balthos moves into new offices, Harrington sends a note of congratulations reflecting their long-term relationship.

The Letter Dear Rob:

Best of luck on the opening of 425 Barton Avenue! Your new offices are just beautiful—a fit setting for Balthos Industries. You must be very proud of all the hard work you and your staff have put in to make the company such a success.

I'm sure that everyone who remembers Balthos' first office in your home especially appreciates how far you've all come.

I wish you all the luck in the world and many more years of success in your new home at #425.

Highest personal regards,

Gardner Harrington

Key Points

- If there is a long-term relationship, let your note reflect it. You have a special perspective on your customer's growth and should mention it.
- Wish your customer luck in his/her new offices.
- Praise the customer for all the hard work that went into the company's growth and success.
- Close with your personal wishes for the customer's good luck and continued success.

12.3 Congratulations on Promotion

Situation Marsha Wingate writes a note of congratulations to a staff member at a customer company who has just been promoted to vice president.

The Letter Dear Howard:

I've just heard the good news! How does it feel to be the new Vice President of Planning for Manchester Industries?

You've made such a difference at Manchester. I know that you've not only positively affected their bottom line, but members of your staff have actually been seen with smiles on their faces during working hours. I'm so glad the company has also recognized and rewarded your talents.

Congratulations and best of luck with your new position.

All my best,

Marsha Wingate

Key Points

- Open informally and let the customer know that you're also excited about the promotion.
- You might want to mention a few reasons why you feel the customer deserves this promotion.
- Close on a positive note offering your congratulations and best wishes.

12.4 Congratulations on Industry Recognition

Situation Rhonda Gibson has just been awarded the prestigious Direct Marketing Society Woman of the Year award. Mel Winthrop, one of Ms. Gibson's company's suppliers, sends this congratulatory note.

The Letter Dear Rhonda:

I wasn't one bit surprised to hear that you've been named Direct Marketing Society's Woman of the Year. I only wondered why it took the industry so long to realize what I've known all along!

Of course, you can expect to see me at the big fund raiser on November 12. Even if the standard chicken and gravy dinner is served, an opportunity to hear one of your celebrated speeches will make it an occasion not to be missed.

Congratulations again from all of us.

Best regards,

Mel Winthrop

Key Points

- An informal tone is appropriate if it is consistent with your existing relationship.
- Share your agreement with the recognition being given your customer.
- You might want to mention some other personal connection you have with the customer or when you expect to meet next.
- In closing, congratulate the customer on receiving the honor.

12.5 Congratulations on Winning a Prize or Honor

Situation Every year the Arkansas farmer's rice cooperative elects a "Friend of the Farmer," someone whose professional efforts have significantly contributed to their product's representation and sales. Howard Casini wins this year's honors. When the announcement of Casini's award is written up in the industry trade papers, one of his suppliers writes a note of congratulations.

The Letter Dear Howard:

I read in this month's *Distribution News* that you've been named this year's "Friend of the Farmer." That's quite an honor and one you readily deserve. You must be very proud of your accomplishments and the recognition you've earned.

I'm happy to hear that you're just as well respected and well liked among your peers as you are among your suppliers8not an easy feat in our business.

Please add my congratulations and good wishes to the many others I'm sure you've received.

All my best,

Ricky Doppleworth

Key Points

- Tell your customer how you heard about the honor. Enthusiastically show that you feel the customer deserved the honor and why.
- Share with your customer that he or she has earned your respect and that of your peers.
- Congratulations and best wishes are an appropriate way to close your letter.

12.6 Congratulations on Retirement

Situation The Director of Marketing at Garson Carroll Company is retiring after 25 years. A sales representative who has been calling on her for several years writes a note to acknowledge the event and extend good wishes.

The Letter Dear Dorothy:

I'll be very sorry to see you leave Garson Carroll Co. this month. Things just won't be the same without you!

I'm sure your co-workers will miss your dedication, creativity, and unfailing good humor. But I'll most miss your terrific jokes whenever I called on you. As a matter of fact, all my other clients will probably miss them too.

Your trip sounds great and I'm sure you'll make good use of all that free time you could never get enough of. We'll all be thinking of you in Naples.

Best wishes,

Ray Harris

Key Points

- If you'll sincerely be sorry to see the customer leave, say so.
- Add a personal touch by including a specific quality that you'll miss.
- Make a positive reference to the retiree's future plans.
- Close with your best wishes for the future.

12.7 Sympathy Note—Version 1

Situation Most of us find sympathy letters difficult to write. It becomes even harder when the note must be written to a business associate. Just remember that the tone of your note should reflect the degree of formality in your relationship. If it has always been business-only, this occasion might not be the right time to act as if you're a close, personal friend. Taking the time to write and offer your personal condolences will still be appreciated by your customer even if your note is brief. One guideline is how much you know about the customer's private life. If you have exchanged personal information about your nonbusiness lives, you may be able to write in a more personal tone.

Bob Jergens is president of a hardware supply company. When his father passes away, a longtime supplier wants to send a sympathy note even though their relationship has always been somewhat formal. When you have been privy to little information about your customer's personal life, a preprinted card can be used as long as a short personal handwritten note is added, or you can just send a short handwritten note. Whichever is used, the note should reflect the tone of the relationship.

The Letter Dear Bob:

Please accept our sympathy on your father's passing.

Everyone at Delafield's joins me in sending you and your family condolences on this sad occasion.

With sincere sympathy,

Laura Hodges

Delafield Tool Company

Key Points

- You can open by offering your sympathy on the occasion.
- Let the customer know that others join you in extending your condolences.
- If you have no personal knowledge of the customer's relationship with the deceased, it would be inappropriate for you to be specific.

12.8 Sympathy Note—Version 2

Situation One of Ron Salko's consulting clients is Cromwell & Co. As their advisor on computer systems and equipment, all his work for the company is channeled through Cromwell's Office Manager, Glenda Pierson. Over the course of Ron's relationship with Cromwell, his conversations with Glenda have included references to her personal life. In fact, he thinks of her as a good "business" friend. When Ron hears that Glenda's husband has unexpectedly died, he writes a handwritten personal note.

The Letter Dear Glenda:

I just heard about Patrick and wanted to offer my condolences to you and your family.

From everything you've told me about him, I'm sure your loss is shared by many. He sounded like a very special man who will be greatly missed. I'm only sorry I never really got to know him, although you were always able to paint such a vibrant picture for me.

Words can say so little in a time of sorrow like this, but please know that I'm thinking of you.

With my sincerest sympathy,

Allan Baum

Key Points

- Offer your customer condolences.
- If you've never met the deceased but have heard about him or her through your customer, share some of the positive qualities you've been told.
- Let the customer know you're thinking of him or her.

12.9 Get-Well Note

Situation One of Ron Palmer's clients has been in an accident that will keep her out of the office for at least four weeks. Since Ron and Michelle have a friendly, informal, and strong working relationship, Ron certainly feels it appropriate to send a get-well note to her home and even include a small gift—a book by an author he knows she likes. Ron understands that missing several weeks of work may make Michelle feel that she is being left out or will fall behind in her responsibilities. In his letter, Ron tries to be reassuring about these sensitive areas. He also wants his note to strengthen their existing relationship and bridge the time Michelle will be out of the office by establishing a time when they will next meet.

The Letter Dear Michelle:

I was so sorry to hear about your accident.

I'm sure the four weeks home will pass much faster than you think—and to help keep your mind off the calendar, I'm sending you the newest Stephen King novel. It's one of those 1000-pagers. If you take your time, you could lose a week or more right there. Of course, I've already read it. In my opinion, it's one of his best. But don't think you can get me to tell you how it ends!

Your office told me you're expected back the week of April 12. You'll probably have a lot to catch up on that week, even though Gary sounds like he has everything under control. If I don't hear from you by the 19th, I'll give you a call. I'd like to continue our conversation about a new direction for next year. The suggestions you made at our last session were very helpful, and I've come up with a plan I think you'll really like. Maybe we'll be able to schedule a meeting later in the month.

In the meantime, make the most of your time at home. It's a pity to have to go to such lengths to get four consecutive weeks off from work. The least you can do is relax and enjoy it.

Get better soon!

Ron Palmer

Key Points

- It's doubtful you would write a get-well letter unless (1) you and your customer have a somewhat informal, friendly relationship and (2) your customer will be out of work for at least a few weeks. A one-week flu would not merit a get well note mailed home.
- Tell the customer you're sorry to hear about the problem.
- Add a light note, such as an anecdote about an amusing or interesting event that happened since the customer has been at home. You might comment on the gift you enclosed. Make sure it is appropriate in price and content—like an inexpensive book, puzzle, or audio tape.
- Use your judgment about whether a gift is appropriate.
- If you know when the customer will be back in the office, refer to the date in terms of when you'll next be in contact.
- Being out of the office for any length of time is often difficult. Let the customer know how you are already planning for their return.
- Close on a light, positive note. Remember to tell the customer to get better soon.

BONUS LETTER

Mary Kay's success story has become a part of American entrepreneurial history. Because the company is so well known and respected, many people write Mary Kay for advice about starting a business of their own.

This letter from Mary Kay herself tells the inspirational story of her success. One can only imagine the excitement and motivation one would get from receiving this response. Many companies would not respond to a request such as this. It is evident, however, that Mary Kay believes her customers and public deserve more.

I received your letter concerning your new business and asking for any advice which I could give you. The founding of Mary Kay Cosmetics is so different from the way in which most companies are begun that it is difficult for me to give advice. You see, I truly believe that, all my life, God was preparing me for this moment and this mission.

Before I founded Mary Kay Cosmetics, I had 25 years experience in direct sales. I had retired -- for one month -- and in preparation for a book I planned to do on women in sales, I made a list of all the good qualities of the companies with which I had been associated, and a list of all those things which I felt could be improved. From these two lists I formulated a marketing plan which I thought would work.

Also, many years before this company was begun, I met the daughter, socially, of the man who originated these formulations. At that point she was just trying to get this product on the market, and I saw 20 women in a room from ages 19 to 70 -- and every one of them had "peaches and cream" complexions. They were her guinea pigs. She told me that she could take credit for every single person's skin in that room except mine. I began to use her product. Within a few months, I could see noticeable changes in my skin for the better. I continued to use it for a period of years. In 1963, after her death, I purchased the formulations. I had always felt she had never gotten the product "off the ground" because her marketing process was in error. I then had the product and the marketing plan -- and beginning this Company was the next step for me. Of course, when we began Mary Kay Cosmetics, I never dreamed it would grow as it has. I couldn't even envision the day when we would be further than Waxahachie -- and we are now international!

My mother used to say to me, "You can do anything in the world that you want to do -- if you want to do it badly enough and you are willing to pay the price." All my life I have lived by this adage, and I combined belief, determination and work with the founding of this Company. I had no administrative background (I left those details to my son), but I put into practice all the experience I had used in direct sales to build a sales organization based on the Golden Rule. I urge you to continue to follow your dream.

Cordially,

Mary Kay
Chairman Emeritus

13
Apology Letters

No matter how hard you and your co-workers try, a busy business will generate its share of customer dissatisfaction.

Whoever or whatever has caused the problem, you must resolve it in a way that is acceptable to the customer. A well-written follow-up note that offers your apologies can show just how concerned you are about your customer's satisfaction and the continuation of your relationship. It reinforces your image as a company that takes a personal interest in the people they do business with.

Of course, your apology note should say that you are sorry for the problem or any inconvenience to the customer. It can highlight the good service you've given the customer in the past. You can add a light touch to soften the reason for writing the note. On the other hand, if the problem was a particularly difficult one, you may want to offer something extra to make up for what happened.

No matter what you say or how you say it, though, make sure you say it right away! How seriously can the customer take your concern and apologies if you wait several weeks to write your note? If you feel an apology note is warranted, make sure it is written so thtat the customer will receive it within one week of the problem.

You may want to review how you've resolved the problem, especially if you've obviously gone out of your way to satisfy the customer. If further action is needed, offer your personal assistance or the name of an individual the customer can contact to follow up. Make the customer feel that there is at least one person at your company to contact directly who will be familiar with the account and available to help.

Key Points

- The most important thing to remember with apology letters is to write them right away. If you wait longer than a few days to mail your letter, you are better off not writing one at all.
- Even if you've been able to satisfactorily resolve the problem, you want the customer to know that you care about more than just making a sale and fulfilling an order, that you want to be the kind of company they want to do business with—and continue doing business with.
- Always try to include something upbeat in your apology note so that the focus of the letter isn't exclusively on what your company did wrong. If you look for something positive to say, you can always find it.
- Offer your personal assistance or that of a specific associate for any further action. Make customers feel as though they have a "friend" at your company.
- If there is a long-term relationship, remind customers of your history and how you've satisfied them in the past.
- Depending on how serious the problem is that prompted your apology letter, you may want to offer the customer something extra to make up for what has happened—free delivery, special pricing, or a gift.

13.1 Apology for a Late Order

Situation Au Chocolat is a shop that provides customized candies for commercial businesses. One of their accounts is The Freemont, a four-star hotel that leaves a hospitality package of fruits, chocolates, and nuts in every room for guests staying two nights or more. When Au Chocolat was given the contract for The Freemont's work, they had been given an approximate quantity of product that they would need to provide each month. When Freemont's orders unexpectedly increased, Au Chocolat ran out of stock and, despite a production rush, was late with their next order to The Freemont. Au Chocolat writes a note to follow up their verbal apology for the delayed order.

The Letter Dear Pierre:

First, let me say congratulations! Your program to increase visitors staying two days or more must be working if I can judge by the quantity of chocolates we're delivering each month. Our original contract estimated 700 boxes monthly and our average over the past four months seems to have crept up to 960.

I appreciate your being so understanding about the late delivery for April, and hope this did not elicit any customer complaints. I'm very sorry if this delay caused you any inconvenience.

We produced 10,000 packages (less the 1,000 shipped to you this week), which should take us through the end of the year. Can we get together to discuss your future plans for this program? I wouldn't want to get caught short again. I will call you next week to set up an appointment.

Sincerely,

Martha Grant

P.S.: I also have some ideas for your hotel shop and special and holiday events that might interest you.

Key Points

- In this instance, the late order can be turned around to indicate a positive trend for the customer's business. Explain that your late order was largely due to their growth.
- Express your apologies for the inconvenience, and thank the customer for being understanding about the situation.
- Tell the customer what you plan to do to prevent a recurrence of the problem.
- Suggest a meeting to review the customer's needs. Show that you are interested in the customer's success and what you can do to contribute to it.
- Close with an upbeat P.S. about a new idea, a future project, or a positive comment indicating a successful and ongoing relationship with the customer.

13.2 Apology for Incorrect Merchandise

Situation General Supply Distributors is a food company supplying fresh fruits and vegetables to Seawind School District. When Seawind schedules a Strawberry Festival, they order specific fruits from GSD rather than whichever fruits are priced best that week. However, when the warehouse men pack Seawind's order, they automatically pack a mix of items specially priced rather than the strawberries, blueberries, and melons requested. When Seawind realizes the mistake, they immediately call GSD who schedules a quick pick-up and redelivery for the next day. I addition, GSD follows up with a letter of apology to the customer.

The Letter Dear Mrs. O'Hara:

I know how upset you must have been to discover that the berries you were looking forward to serving had been substituted with pears and apples. And, of course, you couldn't be expected to have a strawberry festival without strawberries!

By the time you receive this letter you will have received the correct fruit from us and served it to your students. I expect that the fruit and the opening of your festival were a big success.

Most of all, I wanted to extend my personal regrets for having allowed your initial order to be delivered with the wrong fruit. In order to make all our deliveries on time, the loaders sometimes work automatically without taking the time to carefully review the items selected by customers like yourself who have regular, stock orders. I will personally make sure a mistake like this never happens to Seawind again.

The festival sounded like a wonderful idea. Let me know if we can help you with any other special events.

Sincerely,

Martin Bennett

Key Points

- Empathize with how the customer felt to find the wrong merchandise.
- Mention that you promptly switched the incorrect items for the ones ordered.
- Extend your personal apologies for the mistake. Offer to personally make sure that this type of mistake does not happen again.
- Close on a lighter note. Offer your services for future business with the customer. Call attention to your existing relationship and expectations to continue it.

13.3 Apology for a Misplaced Order

Situation

Upon ordering an EZ-UZE Video Recorder from Magic Electronics, a customer is told that the model is out of stock, but expected in stock soon enough to be shipped to arrive for use at his daughter's graduation. Four days before the big event, the customer still has not received the recorder. When Joe calls Magic's to check, no record exists of the order. The Sales Manager acknowledges that the order has been misplaced and no recorder sent. Since the product is now in stock, Magic's offers to send it prepaid overnight delivery. The Sales Manager follows up with a note of apology to create more of a personal connection with his somewhat disgruntled customer.

The Letter

Dear ______:

I'm sure your daughter's graduation ceremony was a memorable event that you'll enjoy again and again on tape. Congratulations from all of us at Magic's Electronics.

While I cannot apologize enough for the problem we had with your order, I am very glad we were able to get the EZ-UZE Recorder to you on time for your family's special occasion.

It would have been of little solace to you that only a handful of the thousands and thousands of orders we process annually get misplaced during processing. We're very glad the problem was resolved satisfactorily since your business is very important to us.

Please let me know if I can be of assistance to you in the future. I've already put you on our special customer's file for advance notice of special sale events and promotions.

Sincerely,

Robert Henshaw
Sales Manager

Key Points

- Try to start your letter on a light, positive note. For example, express your hope that the customer is already enjoying use of the item purchased.
- Apologize for whatever problem your company caused the customer. If appropriate, make sure you also mention that the problem was satisfactorily resolved.
- Include that it is highly unusual for a problem of this type to occur.
- Let customers know that their business is very important to you.
- Offer your personal assistance.
- Close in a way that implies future business from the customer—in this case, adding the customer's name to a special list.

13.4 Apology for Defective Merchandise

Situation RZT Distributors is one of Leslie Electronics' main suppliers of wires and cables. One item in their most recent order included several cases of cables that turned out to be defective. Leslie's Purchasing Agent calls to complain and get the cases replaced.

The Letter Dear ______:

I wish I could tell you that yours was the only problem we have had with our heavy-duty coaxial cables. Unfortunately, your shipment was just one of what must have been an entire lot of defective merchandise.

Since this was discovered on Tuesday, we've been trying to contact all customers who received stock from Lot 42. I'm very sorry that you contacted us about the problem before we were able to get to you.

As I explained to you on the phone, I've already issued a replacement order scheduled for Tuesday delivery. Our driver will pick up the defective boxes then too.

I know that this type of problem can also create delivery difficulties with your customers. Please accept my deepest apologies for any inconvenience this may have caused you. If there's any way we can be of assistance to you, let me know.

Sincerely,

Sales Manager

P.S.: We have already instituted a test procedure to make sure we identify problems like this one before our customers are affected.

Key Points

- Be straightforward with your customer about the problem merchandise.
- Let the customer know what you plan to do.
- Apologize for any problems caused by the defective merchandise.
- Show how concerned you are by offering to assist the customer in any other way required.

13.5 Apology for Poor Service

Situation Misplaced X-Rays, double-booked appointments, a doctor who runs late for appointments—all these are problems facing Claudia Regan with Dr. Casals, a periodontist recommended by her regular dentist. Finally, despite the recommendation, Mrs. Regan tells Dr. Casals' secretary to cancel the remainder of her appointments. Two days later she receives a letter from Dr. Casals.

The Letter Dear Mrs. Regan:

Marsha told me that you called on Tuesday to cancel the series of appointments that we had set up for your periodonture work. I understand that some difficulties with my office prompted the cancellations.

Please understand that I was unaware of any problems prior to my conversation yesterday with Marsha, when I noticed that your name had been removed from this month's bookings. While an abbreviated version of your message was relayed to me, I would greatly appreciate the opportunity to speak to you directly. I offer my apologies for any way you have been inconvenienced, although I'd prefer to apologize in person.

I am also hoping that, by hearing about the specific difficulties you've had with my office, I can make adjustments to prevent problems like this in the future. My patients are all important to me, and your dissatisfaction causes me considerable distress.

I am in my office on Fridays from 9 to 12 for paperwork and phone consultations. I would greatly appreciate your phoning me then.

Sincerely,

Bernard Casals, M.D.

Key Points

- Review your understanding of the customer's current status.
- Ask for the opportunity to discuss the situation with the customer in person or over the phone.
- Offer your apologies for what has happened.
- Request the customer's help in educating you so that you can prevent a future repetition of similar problems.
- Let customers know that they are important to you.
- While you may not be able to ensure future business with the customer, try to create an opportunity for future contact.
- In closing, let customers know you would like them to call and when you will be available.

13.6 Apology for an Abrupt Change in Policy

Situation When policy changes come suddenly or without notice, customers are often left confused, disappointed, or angry. Companies should plan changes of policy well in advance and notify customers whenever possible. When a problem arises because of an abrupt change of policy, customers should be treated fairly.

The Letter

Dear ______:

We are sorry to hear that you were confused about our recent change in policy.

As of June 16, we are no longer offering free shipping on credit card orders. Our free shipping for prepayment only applies to orders that are accompanied by a check or money order.

Because of this change, a $6.45 shipping charge was added to your credit card order.

Since this policy change was so recent, and because you are such a good customer, we will credit your charge card account for the shipping charge. A copy of that credit voucher is attached.

As of this date, however, the new policy stands in effect.

Again, we are sorry to have caused you any inconvenience.

Sincerely,

Customer Service Manager

Key Points

- Tell the customer why you are writing.
- Explain the change in policy.
- Apologize for the confusion caused by the policy change.
- Waive the new policy or make a concession to show customers that they come first.
- Restate the new policy and the date it went into effect.
- Apologize again.

13.7 Apology for a Change in Personnel Requested

Situation *Today's Parenting* is a popular magazine primarily read by mothers of newborns to 8-year-olds. The advertising sales staff consists of telephone sales representatives who develop their own client lists. When the top salesperson leaves, her client list is divided among the other reps. Although the majority of advertisers are satisfied with their new representatives, one in particular is not. Dan Penner, *Today's Parenting*'s Advertising Sales Manager writes to the customer about this unavoidable change.

The Letter Dear Ms. Carrera:

I too wish that Julie Connors had not decided to move to Montana with her new husband and leave *Today's Parenting*. She was highly valued here as a top professional and an irreplaceable friend. We all miss her.

Before she left, however, Julie reviewed each and every one of her accounts with the salesperson assigned to take it over. In your case, I am personally aware of the time spent reviewing Kidstuff's history and current advertising needs and expectations with Bob Ryan, Julie's successor.

I am sorry that your initial meeting with Bob did not inspire your confidence. You had been working with Julie for three years and a period of adjustment to a new rep should be expected—especially since you and Julie worked so well together.

While Bob Ryan has only been with us a short time, he has an exceptional background and an impressive sheaf of recommendations. Julie hand-picked him to handle your account and felt that he'd not only be able to take over where she left off, but even surpass what she was able to do for you.

Would you be willing to give Bob a little more time to instill that same confidence in you? If you insist on our switching your account, then, of course, it will be done. I believe, though, that if you work with Bob for another few weeks, you'll be glad you did.

Think it over and let me know your decision. If you'd like to discuss your specific concerns with me, I'll be here all week.

Sincerely,

Dan Penner
Advertising Sales Manager

Key Points

- Express your regrets that the personnel requested is not available to customer.
- Let the customer know that the person now assigned to work on the account has been hand-picked and well trained.
- Validate the customer's feelings of discomfort with the change.
- Offer your support of the new personnel and their abilities.
- Appeal to the customer to work with this person a little longer but also offer an alternative.
- Close by stating your willingness to talk further about the customer's concerns and ultimately to go along with the customer's wishes.

13.8 Apology Letter for Repeated Errors

Situation Sign-On manufactures signs and other display pieces for the business place. Despite an excellent reputation for high-quality work and prompt delivery, they now have a problem with Ronway Hobby Shops because three of the last six jobs done for Ronway have not met their specifications in some way. In two cases, Sign-On was out of stock of the fire engine red paper Ronway had requested as background. In the third instance, Sign-On mistakenly produced a 3 × 5-inch sign instead of the desired 4 × 5 inches. Although Sign-On's Order Manager had verbally apologized for these errors, Bob Bender, Sign-On's president now writes Ronway a note of apology.

The Letter Dear Mr. Ronway:

I wanted to personally apologize for Sign-On's mishandling of your recent orders. I hope that our history of prompt, accurate, and effective sign producing will persuade you to give us another chance to work with you.

By way of explanation, our growth has necessitated new staff who are not yet familiar with the importance of meeting all Ronway's sign specifications. They apparently placed an emphasis on meeting your delivery date, rather than your request for color or size. We've already instituted a more extensive training period for new hires to familiarize them with all the needs of our regular customers.

Can we try to compensate you for any displeasure or inconvenience this may have caused you by fulfilling your next order at no charge? We have plenty of Ronway's red paper in stock now. Just send the next order to my attention so that I can notify Accounting of the special handling.

Sincerely,

Robert Bender
President

Key Points

- Apologize for the mistakes your company has made. Remind the customer of the good work you've done in the past.
- You may want to explain what caused the errors and what has been changed to prevent them from happening in the future.
- If this is a good and long-time customer, you may want to offer something special to make up for the problems. An offer like this also works to maintain the continuity of your relationship with the customer.

13.9 Apology for an Unpopular Company Position

Situation Companies establish policies so that they can conduct business consistently and fairly. Sometimes a policy, when misunderstood by a customer, can cause ill feelings. If the policy cannot be changed, a thorough explanation must be made to the customer.

The Letter Dear ______:

Thank you for your letter expressing your displeasure with our quantity pricing policy.

We are sorry that you are unhappy with this policy. We hope we can explain our position.

As I understand it, you purchased 1000 imprinted pens on August 11 and reordered an additional 2500 on August 29. For both orders, you were charged 24 cents per pen, which is our pricing for orders of 1000-3499 pens. You requested that your second order be billed at 19 cents per pen, which is our 3500-4999 price. We denied your request and billed you at the 2500 quantity price.

Let me explain why we could not honor your request. Our quantity pricing schedule is based on manufacturing economies, that is, on our ability to imprint large numbers of pens with one set-up of the press. An order of 1000 pens and a second order of 2500 pens requires two separate set-ups and costs us significantly more than a single order of 3500 pens. When we can save money because of quantity, we are happy to pass those savings on to our customers. Hence, our quantity pricing schedule.

If you had placed an order for 3500 pens at one time, you would have automatically been billed at 19 cents per pen.

While we would like to honor your request, we cannot since we would actually lose money on your order. I'm sure you can understand that a business cannot operate at a loss.

Again, we apologize for any inconvenience or misunderstanding that our quantity pricing policy has caused you. You are an important customer and we value your business.

I've enclosed a coupon worth $25 off your next order. It's our way of saying that your satisfaction is really important to us.

Sincerely,

Sales Manager

Key Points

- Thank customers for their communication and apologize for the displeasure.
- Restate the problem to show that you are concerned and have looked into the situation.
- Explain why the request cannot be granted.
- Tell customers that you value their business.
- Offer some token to show your desire to keep the customer happy.

Note: If a policy is consistently causing your company customer service problems, consider changing it or presenting your policy in clearer language.

14

Thank You Letters

Thank you letters are the "good manners" of business correspondence. They are an important courtesy and show your social etiquette as well as your respect for the customer.

Whenever in doubt about sending a thank you letter, send it. You can never send too many, but neglecting this social obligation can damage your relationship.

Besides being the right thing to do, thank you letters offer the opportunity to strengthen the goodwill between you and your client. Write the letter in an informal, personal manner. Try to convey your enthusiasm and appreciation in the tone of the letter. Whenever possible, recall the favor, gift, or good deed, and tell the recipient what it meant to you.

Key Points

- Keep the thank you note casual, friendly, and short.
- Whenever you think of sending a thank you note, do it.
- Show your appreciation with a friendly, enthusiastic tone.
- Specifically cite the good deed, favor, or gift.
- Keep the letter concise.

14.1 Thank You for a First Order

Situation Many companies work very hard to acquire a new customer and then neglect taking advantage of the perfect opportunity to start the relationship on a positive note—the first order. When the initial order is received, a letter should immediately be sent to the new customer offering thanks and cementing the new relationship with positive expectations and goodwill.

The Letter Dear ______:

We have just received your purchase order #1.382 and would like to thank you for ordering from York Publishing.

It's always a pleasure to welcome a new customer. We work very hard to create and publish the best publications on health and fitness. But, without the help of distributors like you, our publications would not receive the exposure they merit.

Jim Anderson, your sales representative, tells me that your firm has an excellent reputation and provides service to the entire Northwest, a territory where we can use all the assistance we can get. I'm excited about our association and its potential for both firms.

Your order is currently being processed, and you should receive it within 10 days.

Thanks again for your first order. If I can be of any service, do not hesitate to call.

Sincerely,

Nancy Goethe
General Manager

Key Points

- Confirm the order and thank the customer.
- Share your feelings about how important the customer is to your success.
- If you know something positive about the new customer, mention it. Everyone likes to hear a compliment, and there's no better way to start a relationship and build goodwill.
- State your expectations of continued business.
- Make sure that the initial order is processed efficiently and expedited. Your friendly response must be backed up with excellent service—especially on the first order.

14.2 Thank You for Continued Business

Situation Loyal customers deserve recognition. It is to the benefit of suppliers to thank customers for their continued business. While any time is the right time to express your appreciation, it is often convenient to do so on the customer's anniversary date.

The Letter

Dear ______:

Time flies. That's what they say, and now I know it's true!

While reviewing your files, I realized that it has been five years since we processed your first order for packaging materials. I well remember how we worked together to meet the minimum. And today you're one of our largest customers, ordering by the truckload.

I'm writing to say thank you. First, for the terrific business that you give us. Second, for the professional way you conduct your business. All of us here at Worldwide are impressed with the organized and efficient manner in which your orders are placed.

I'd just like to say one last thing. We've watched your business grow from a start-up to an industry leader over the past five years, and it couldn't have happened to a more deserving, dedicated group of people.

Again, thank you for your continued business.

Sincerely,

Everly Grosset
President

Key Points

- Begin the letter in an interesting, informal manner.
- Thank the customer for the business you have received.
- Relate some anecdote or remembrance that shows you are personally aware of the customer.
- Restate your thanks.

14.3 Thank You for a Large Order

Situation As soon as this firm wins the contract for a large project, they write a letter thanking the new client for the award. The letter is designed to let the client know how pleased they are about the project and to reassure them of having made the right decision. It also lets the client know what will happen next.

The Letter Dear ______:

We have just received word of your decision to accept our bid for the Evergreen project. I'd like to personally thank you for your confidence in us.

The entire staff is very excited about working with you. We all feel strongly that this is an exciting opportunity to design and build something that will benefit a great many people for years to come. There's nothing I can think of that would be more challenging and ultimately satisfying for us to be a part of.

It looks as though the time schedule you established will be no problem, but I would like to meet with you and your key people to review Evergreen's first stage before we give the go-ahead to all departments.

Let me know what dates are most convenient for you and we'll make ourselves available.

Sincerely,

Executive Vice President

Key Points

- Thank the customer for choosing you.
- Let the customer know how excited you and your staff are about this project.
- Include at least one reason for your excitement other than the financial benefit—the chance to work with the customer, to create something special, to do what you enjoy most or do best.
- Reassure the customer that you have everything under control and describe the next step.

BONUS LETTER

Good manners and personal interest certainly do count! What customer wouldn't be pleased to receive this acknowledgment from Mary Kay in response to a note about product satisfaction.

This relationship-building thank you note will make the customer feel important and valued.

Customer Appreciates Product

I have received your most complimentary letter concerning the results you are experiencing in using Mary Kay Cosmetics, and I'm so delighted to know of this! Millions of users around the world attest to the fact our skin care program is the one and only for them—and we're so happy you feel the same way.

Thank you for telling us of your pleasant association with [the Mary Kay sales representative]. We are blessed with many such wonderful people, and we are most grateful. Your taking the time to write us to compliment her so highly was so very nice.

Wonderful people like you have made our company the success it is today, and WE APPRECIATE YOU!

Cordially,

Mary Kay
Chairman Emeritus

cc: [The sales representative]

BONUS LETTER

Campbell Soup Company strengthens customer relationships with every opportunity. In the following letter, the customer service representative lets the customer know that the company is happy to receive customer comments whether they are good or bad.

In addition to Campbell Soup Company's expressed appreciation for these compliments, the company uses this opportunity to offer a coupon and a gift of recipe suggestions.

Campbell Soup Company

May 23, 1991

Dear

Thank you for taking the time to give us such kind and thoughtful comments. We appreciate hearing both positive and negative comments from our consumers, and yours were particularly rewarding.

For over 100 years, we at Campbell's have worked to make the best products available at an economical price. Compliments like yours help us feel that we are achieving that goal.

Since you are interested in good food, I am enclosing a coupon for one of our Campbell products and some of our favorite recipe suggestions. I hope you enjoy them.

Sincerely,

Consumer Correspondent

14.4 Thank You for the Business Referral

Situation Business derived from word of mouth referrals can be one of the best ways to build your business. While it is difficult to promote customer referrals (other than by providing an excellent product and service), you can tell a referrer how much you appreciate the good word. A simple thank you note can go a long way to ensure that you will be recommended again.

The Letter Dear Bob:

I just received a phone call from Terri Jones of Southside Foods asking for a quote on designing their next annual report. Terri said that you recommended us and told her how pleased everyone at Chemical Services was with our last project.

I'd like to thank you for the referral. Your kind words have given us the chance to work with one of the largest public companies in the area. This opportunity can possibly give us the national exposure we've been seeking.

Let's get together next week for lunch. I'd like to thank you in person. I'll call you in a day or so to see when you're available.

Sincerely,

Key Points

- Explain how you learned of the referral. Offer your thanks for the effort on your behalf.
- If the referral has special meaning to your company, say so.
- Thank the referrer again and, when appropriate, offer to meet so that you can express your thanks in person.

14.5 Thank You for a Referral Who Became a Customer

Situation When a customer makes a referral, he or she should be thanked immediately. If the referral becomes a customer, the referrer should be told and thanked again. Billions of Buttons has worked hard to convince Drescher Clothes to buy from them. When the first order is received, a thank you letter is sent to the referrer.

The Letter

Dear ______:

Thank you! Thank you! Thank you!

This morning, when I opened my mail, I was delighted to find an order from Drescher Clothes. This is our first order from Drescher, and I owe it all to you.

If you remember back in January, you were kind enough to introduce me to Hank Drescher and say a few positive things about Billions of Buttons. Since then, Hank and I have met a number of times. I really enjoy Hank and am very impressed with what he has accomplished at Drescher. This first order means that Hank was equally impressed by our capabilities.

Your faith in us and willingness to refer BOB to your associates makes all our hard work pay off. If there is any way I can reciprocate, please let me know. For the time being, however, let me restate how much we appreciate your efforts in your behalf.

Sincerely,

P.S.: As you know, next week is the annual convention. I'll be there Monday and Tuesday. Let's get together for dinner. I'll call you to see which night is good for you.

Key Points

- Offer an enthusiastic thank you.
- By describing the circumstances of the first order, you show how important it is to you and make the referrer feel good.
- Sincerely state what the referral means to you.
- Offer to return the favor if possible.

14.6 Thank You for a Favor

Situation Businesspeople help their associates in a multitude of ways. A short note expressing thanks shows your appreciation for the favor in a professional manner. When people extend themselves to provide assistance, they expect to be thanked. A letter sent after a favor formally states your gratitude and leaves a positive impression.

The Letter Dear ______:

Thank you!

I've just received the financial report you ran for me on Zest Vests. The information it revealed will be extremely important to our negotiations.

Without your assistance, I don't know how I could have found out this background data. And I know I could never have gotten it as fast as you did.

Thanks again. I hope I'll be able to return the favor soon.

Sincerely,

P.S.: If you incurred any costs, please let me know. I'll immediately send you a check to cover them.

Key Points

- Thank the individual who has done you a favor.
- Explain why the favor was important to you.
- Offer to reciprocate if possible.
- When appropriate, volunteer to reimburse the individual for any expenses.

14.7 Thank You for a Donation

Situation Charitable organizations raise revenue with which to do their good works through fund-raising activities. When a gift is received, it is the organization's responsibility to thank the donor for the donation. The "thank you" acknowledges the gift's receipt and expresses the charity's gratitude for the donor's generosity.

The Letter Dear ______:

I am writing to personally thank you for the generous gift you sent to help us with our annual fund raiser.

It is through the caring of individuals such as yourself that Guardian Charities can help young people in crisis in the Jacksonville area.

As you know, Guardian has provided counseling services to children of alcoholic families for over a decade. Counseling is offered at no charge to families in financial need. We have helped hundreds of children, with nowhere to turn, cope with their parents' drinking problems and often emotional and physical abuse.

Recently, Tom Handerson returned to Guardian for a visit. He was a youth-at-risk when he first came to Guardian eight years ago. Constantly in trouble at school and with the law, Tom could have been one of those negative statistics—a juvenile offender with drug and alcohol addiction. Instead, he is an example of a young man determined to make something of his life. Tom is a sophomore at Dowling College, works as a custodian at the local YMCA to pay for his schooling, and is actively involved in fund raising for Guardian.

For Tom and all of us at Guardian we want to thank you again and say that your help really makes an important difference.

Sincerely,

Director

P.S.: I've enclosed a flyer describing our upcoming antique auction. It will be a great fun event, and we'd love to see you there.

Key Points

- Thank the donor for the gift.
- Express how the gift will be used to further the goals of the organization.
- Relate a special example of the charitable activities directly related to the gifts of donors.
- Restate your thanks.

14.8 Thank You for Volunteering

Situation Clarkville Hospital's annual fund-raising event is over and it's time to thank all the volunteers for their assistance. Nancy Stein, the event's chairperson, has decided to write personal thank you notes to each volunteer.

The Letter Dear ______:

As chairperson of the Clarkville Hospital Annual Golf Outing, I'd like to thank you for the outstanding job you did as head of the prize committee.

Everyone has remarked about the quantity, quality, and diversity of the prizes. And when they learned that the prizes were all given by organizations as donations, they were even more impressed.

This year's event raised more money for the hospital than any previous outing. Our success was due largely to the efforts of volunteers like you.

We all realize how much time you contributed. Thank you again for the tremendous job.

Sincerely,

P.S.: I'll call you in about a week to discuss next year. As you know, planning begins almost immediately. And we're counting on your help!

Key Points

- Offer thanks for the time and effort expended.
- If possible, describe why the individual's work was so appreciated.
- If the event was a success, say so. Try to tie the volunteer's efforts to that success.
- Thank the volunteer and, when appropriate, ask for help in the future.

14.9 Thank You for the Suggestion

Situation A customer of Bloomfield's Department Store has made a suggestion to a salesperson. The store manager writes the customer a letter thanking her for the idea.

The Letter Dear ______:

My name is Bill Roberts, and I am manager of Bloomfield's Department Store. Jon Jackson, a salesperson in our men's shirt department, has told me about a suggestion that you made on a recent visit to our store.

Jon said that, while you were browsing through the shirt department, four separate salespeople came over to ask if you needed help. Naturally, you found this excessive attention disturbing. You appreciated the good customer service, but the overkill made shopping uncomfortable. Your idea was for the first salesperson to approach a customer to give them a colored label to wear so that other salespeople would know that the customer had already been helped by the "red" salesperson.

I do not know if this will work, but I really appreciate your relating your feelings to us. Sometimes we think we are doing an excellent job providing service, when in actuality the opposite is occurring.

I'll be meeting with the department managers next week and will bring up your idea. We hope to solve the problem before your next visit to Bloomfield's.

Thanks again for your suggestion.

Sincerely,

Store Manager

P.S.: Enclosed is a $20 gift certificate. Please use it the next time you're in Bloomfield's. We look forward to seeing you soon.

Key Points

- Explain the reason you are writing.
- Thank the customer for the suggestion and say something about it to show that you are aware of the idea.
- You do not need to promise that you will use the idea—just state that you will seriously consider it.
- When possible, offer the customer a token of your thanks. Customers who go out of their way to make suggestions deserve special attention and/or treatment.

14.10 Thank You for a Suggestion That Has Been Implemented

Situation Pier 21 restaurant has taken action on a suggestion made by one of their customers. The idea was an instant success. The restaurant owner has decided to write the customer a thank you letter and offer her a complimentary dinner.

The Letter Dear ______:

The next time you visit Pier 21 Restaurant, you'll find something new on the menu. We've taken your advice and added a special tasting plate of our gourmet appetizers.

Your suggestion has really stirred things up here. We all loved your concept of adding a tasting plate. But when it came to deciding which appetizers to include, no one was in agreement. After at least a week of discussion, it was finally decided. The new tasting plate, priced at $12.95, includes six mouth-watering appetizers. I won't tell you which ones now; you'll have to come in yourself to find out.

And your dinner is on us! It's our way of saying thanks for the suggestion. Now our loyal customers and first-time visitors can sample our renowned appetizers before their meals.

Key Points

- Enthusiastically thank the customer for the suggestion.
- Explain how the suggestion has benefited the business.
- Offer the customer a gift or token as a thank you.

14.11 Thank You for Helping Our Business Grow

Situation Evans Electrical writes to a special customer, for no other reason than to say thank you for being part of their success.

The Letter Dear ______:

Over the past decade, Evans Electrical has grown to be the largest electrical contractor in South Chicago. We've achieved the goals that our founder, Eric Evans, established in 1970, the year Evans first opened its doors. That goal was "to furnish quality work and excellent service to the builders of a new Chicago."

But we did not accomplish our goals alone. As one of our most important customers, thanks must be given to you. Without your faith in our ability, we would not be where we are today.

All of us at Evans want to extend our heartfelt thanks for your business over all these years. We look forward to the future and to our mutual successes.

Sincerely,

President

Key Points

- Describe your special relationship with the customer.
- Offer a sincere expression of your thanks.
- When appropriate, recount an anecdote that portrays the relationship's positive history.

14.12 Thank You for Considering Our Product (Even Though We Didn't Get the Sale)

Situation When customers review a product but decline to purchase, you still have the opportunity to build goodwill and possibly a future sale. A letter thanking customers for their consideration of your product and extending a final special offer can be effective.

The Letter Dear ______:

Thank you for ordering PC Billing, the complete accounting software system for small businesses.

We've received the returned demo along with your note telling us of your decision not to purchase at this time.

We certainly respect your decision. However, we thought you'd be interested in the following facts:

- 78 percent of PC Billing users report that the software paid for itself within two months of purchase.
- 85 percent said that the built-in statement program cut payables by 15 days.
- 92 percent of our users relate significant reductions in the overall hours of their accounting departments after converting to PC Billing.

Remember that there's absolutely no risk with PC Billing. Order it and use it for 30 days in your operation. If it doesn't streamline your accounting, return it to us and owe nothing!

We hope you'll give PC Billing a try soon.

Sincerely,

Customer Service

P.S.: Any order received before September 21 will be discounted 10 percent. So call in your order today!

Key Points

- Thank the customer for trying your product.
- Take this opportunity to reveal some selling points that may have been overlooked by the customer.
- Propose a special discount that may make the customer reconsider the decision not to buy.
- Close with an open-ended offer for the customer to purchase at some future date.

15

Holiday Letters

To most people, "The Holidays" means the December holidays—Chanukah, Christmas, and New Year's. And traditionally, sending holiday wishes usually means a season's greetings card or gift sent at that time of year—along with countless others.

But holiday letters can mean much more and can be used to boost your customer service efforts all 12 months of the year.

Some companies ask for customers' birthdays at their first purchase and then send a happy birthday note each year. This is also a perfect opportunity to offer a special gift to make your customer feel really special. Everyone likes to be remembered on his or her birthday, and few of us expect a birthday surprise from a business associate or supplier.

What about summer, fall, winter, and spring? In some businesses, the start of a new season is the perfect reason for sending a special note or letter to their customers. And on, say, a Tuesday in September, your greeting won't be competing with hundreds of others for your customer's attention.

Thanksgiving, anniversaries, a special day to honor your customers, or some other event you've created can be reason enough to send holiday wishes. A holiday is your chance to tell customers that you:

- Are thinking of them.
- Appreciate all they do for you throughout the year,.
- Hope your relationship strengthens and grows.
- Have something special or new you want to announce.

The opportunities are endless. Just how inventive you can be is up to you and your imagination.

A holiday note can be warmer, friendlier, and more informal than other customer correspondence. While the tone of these letters should take their lead from the type of business you're in and the type of relationship you have with your customers, you may be able to add a more personal, lighter, or more humorous touch than usual. Be careful, though, not to present yourself or your company in a way that will make your customers uncomfortable or ill at ease.

Just a few examples of holiday letters are included in this chapter, but with a little bit of time and effort you will come up with many creative ideas of your own.

Key Points

- Step away from the pack by using holidays all year long to support your customer service efforts.
- Recognizing your customers on personal celebration days, such as birthdays or wedding anniversaries, may be appropriate too.
- You can turn any day or event into a reason to let your customers know you're thinking of them and appreciate their loyalty.
- Here's an opportunity to use your imagination. Put it to your best advantage!

15.1 New Year Wishes

Situation Rather than allow the message to get lost among the many Christmas and Chanukah cards sent during the holiday season, the president of Sweepers sends new year's wishes in this note to customers.

The Letter

Dear Customer:

At the turn of the new year, the entire staff of Sweepers wishes everyone at The Highlands Group health, happiness, and success in the coming year.

This time of year is not only an occasion for celebration but for reflection as well. We'd like to use this opportunity to thank you for your patronage. We hope to continue serving you throughout this year and for many years to come.

All the best throughout the new year.

President
For All of Us at Sweepers

Key Points

- Your tone in this note can be warm and informal. Emphasize the existing relationship between you and your customer.
- Extend wishes for health, happiness, success, or whatever you'd like for your customer, on your own behalf and on behalf of your staff.
- Use the letter to let customers know how much you appreciate their business.
- Close by offering warm wishes for the coming year.

15.2 Christmas/Chanukah Wishes

Situation

Back in the days when life was simpler, individuals and businesses sent out Christmas or Chanukah wishes during the holiday season. But today, with the diversity of people in the workplace, a general, nonreligious greeting is considered more appropriate and less problematic.

If you know recipients well enough, you should address them by name. In these instances, the cards should have personal handwritten salutations and signatures.

If you're sending several hundred cards to customers, it is still advisable to handwrite your signature. But if your customers are in the thousands or tens of thousands, you might want to have your signature printed on the card. Whatever you choose, try to keep as much of a personal touch as possible.

Your message can be short and simple.

The Letter

May your year be filled with peace and love.

Wishing you health and happiness during the holiday season.

Key Points

- Keep the greeting nonsectarian.
- When possible, personally address and sign the greeting.
- It's a good idea to tie your company's products or services into the message or graphics if possible. By subtly using your products, logo, or slogan in the design of the greeting, you can tastefully build your image.

15.3 Birthday Wishes

Situation A local shoe store keeps the birth dates of all customers and sends birthday notes to them each year with a special gift.

The Letter Dear Miss Handler:

Why is April 10 an important day at Shoe Stall?

It gives us a chance to wish you a *happy birthday* and to thank you for shopping with us during the past year!

We hope you have a very special day—and as our gift, we've enclosed this discount certificate in the amount of $20. You can use it with your next purchase or any time before December 31, 19____.

Once again, have a wonderful birthday! We look forward to seeing you again soon.

With Best Birthday Wishes,

Store Manager

Key Points

- You can use a nontraditional opening with this type of personal customer letter.
- Tie in your birthday wishes with a special offer or gift that will induce the customer to purchase from you in the near future.
- Close warmly, extending birthday wishes to your customer.

15.4 Business Anniversary Wishes

Situation It is your business's fifth anniversary. One of their suppliers, Webcor, writes a congratulatory note for the special occasion. It's a personal note that also reinforces Webcor's place as part of your business "family."

The Letter Dear John:

How does it feel to be five years old? I'll bet you can hardly believe it's been that long since Vistassist opened its doors!

Even though Webcor wasn't with you from the start, I know how far you've come in a very short time—and how proud you must be when you look around and see what you've accomplished.

I want to offer my good wishes on this very special occasion. Happy anniversary and best wishes for many more rewarding years to come.

To your continued success,

Rob Kendall
President

Key Points

- Use a friendly, informal tone in a congratulatory note like this one.
- Compliment your customer on the accomplishments an anniversary represents.
- Extend good wishes for the customer's continued success.

15.5 Personal Anniversary Wishes

Situation A tradition at the accounting firm of O'Brien & Associates is sending congratulatory notes to clients whose anniversary dates are known. Even a brief note strengthens the company's image as a firm that takes a personal interest in its clients. The tone of each note is determined by the level of formality between the O'Brien associate and the client, as well as the personalities involved. The relationship between Donald Evans and his clients, Marsha and John, allows for the following light, humorous note.

The Letter Dear Marsha and John:

Congratulations on your tenth wedding anniversary!

May your assets and your years together continue to flourish and grow. We'll keep on doing our part; you do yours.

All our best,

Don Evans

Key Points

- Congratulate your customer on the occasion.
- If possible, connect the event with the service you provide.
- Humor adds a nice touch to your good wishes if it can be tastefully done. When in doubt about the appropriateness of your message, *don't* use it. A straightforward note of congratulations is appreciated too.

15.6 Thanksgiving Wishes

Situation Worldwide Communications Company is a telephone company that has aggressively pursued new subscribers over the past year. At Thanksgiving time, the company sends out a letter of appreciation to all new customers.

The Letter Dear Customer:

At this time of year, when Americans young and old are reflecting on what they are grateful for in their lives, WWCI wants to thank you for joining our family of customers over the past year. We appreciate your confidence in us and will continue to give you the best telephone service possible in the future.

We wish you and your family good health, happiness, and much to be thankful for during the holiday season and the upcoming year.

Happy Thanksgiving,

Key Points

- Tell your customer that, in keeping with the Thanksgiving season, you want to offer thanks for their patronage.
- Wish customers, their families, and/or their staff the best during the holiday season and coming year.
- You may want to send out Thanksgiving wishes instead of the more commonly used Christmas/Chanukah or New Year's greetings.

15.7 Seasonal Wishes

Situation Mr. Frosty's Snow Removal Service clears private parking lots for commercial establishments. A letter is sent to all customers during the fall to wish them a successful season and remind them of the services Mr. Frosty's provides.

The Letter Dear ______:

We want to take this opportunity to wish you a very successful fall season. But before we know it, winter will be here! And this year, even the *Farmer's Almanac* predicts a cold and stormy season.

Whether you're concerned about your employees getting to work or your customers' ability to shop, don't you feel better knowing your parking lots will be automatically cleared no matter how bad the weather?

At Mr. Frosty's Snow Removal Service, our trucks and de-icers are always ready and able to service our contract customers early enough to meet their needs. And this year our new Super 2000 machines will easily be able to handle the extra-deep drifts in half the time.

Mr. Frosty's has been clearing Ridgefield Mall's lots since 19____, and we look forward to serving you this year and in the winters to come.

Sincerely,

President

Key Points

- Offer your good wishes for a successful season.
- Tie the season in to your company and what it provides to your customers.
- Remind customers of your relationship and history. Let customers know how glad you are to provide service, now and in the future.

15.8 Seasonal Tie-in to a Product or Service

Situation Sparkle, Inc., a commercial cleaning company, writes to all customers to encourage an appointment for their spring clean-up services.

The Letter Dear Customer:

The days are getting longer, the weather warmer, and buds are beginning to adorn the bare branches. In fact, spring is right around the corner.

What does that mean to *you*?

It means that spring clean-up time is here again and that Sparkle, Inc. is available for all your office and showroom needs. Would you like your...

Windows washed?
Drapes and upholstery cleaned?
Floors scraped and refinished?
Metal fixtures polished?
Woodwork polished and repaired?
Display pieces refurbished or updated?

Whatever your office or showroom requires to look ready for the spring season, Sparkle, Inc. will be happy to handle—quickly, efficiently, and economically.

Help your business "spring" ahead with the kind of shine that Sparkle, Inc. can provide. Call us at 555-7600 to set up an appointment and find out about our special *Spring Ahead Discount Packages.*

We look forward to hearing from you soon.

Sincerely,

Key Points

- Conjure up images of the season for your customer.
- Tell customers what the season means in the context of your product or service.
- Announce what you are offering and what you would like the customer to do next.
- Make a special offer that ties into the seasonal slant of your letter.

16
Appreciation Letters

Studies have shown that the single greatest motivator of people is not money, power, or sex. What makes people act? What is the most powerful motivator? The answer is recognition. People want to feel appreciated for their efforts. By telling people that they make a difference, you reaffirm their self-worth and build their self-esteem.

Appreciation letters are an excellent way to bolster your relationship with a client. They show customers that you are a human being who recognizes their importance and value.

Like thank you letters, appreciation letters can be written in a casual, informal manner. In fact, they may even be handwritten on your personal or business stationery.

Keep your appreciation letter brief, but do not forget to mention the specific kindness, assistance, or effort for which you are writing.

Avoid overstating or exaggerating your appreciation. By expressing your genuine feelings, you will project your warm, heartfelt thanks.

Key Points

- By showing your appreciation to a customer for business or assistance, you tap the powerful motivational force of recognition and build goodwill.
- Keep your letter informal and brief.
- Express your true feelings; avoid hyperbole.

16.1 Complimenting a Company Employee

Situation When a customer writes a letter complimenting one of Gardening World's employees, the store manager writes a follow-up letter of appreciation. This is an excellent opportunity to let customers know how important they are.

The Letter Dear ______:

We just received your kind note complimenting Ruth Thompson for her attentive service on your recent visit to Gardening World.

We truly appreciate the time you took to tell us about Ruth. It's unusual for a customer to make the effort to let us know when something positive has happened. Your letter tells us a lot about Ruth, but also says a great deal about you too. I'll bet that your enthusiastic attitude contributes to people's eagerness to assist you—at Gardening World and elsewhere.

Thank you again for your acknowledgment of Ruth's efforts. She is one of our best salespeople and really has a great background in horticulture. I know that your praise will mean a great deal to her. And thank you too for shopping at Gardening World. We hope to continue to be your first choice for plants and gardening supplies.

Sincerely,

General Manager

Key Points

- Acknowledge the customer's compliment.
- Let the customer know that the note is unusual—and most appreciated.
- Express your agreement that the employee deserves praise.
- Tell the customer that you will inform the employee of the compliment.
- End by inviting the customer to shop with you again.

16.2 Complimenting a Company Policy

Situation Davidson and Greerly receive many letters regarding their vanguard efforts in environmental conservation. Because this project is so important to the company, Adam Greerly always writes a personal appreciation letter in response to comments and correspondence received. The customers who write are usually surprised and pleased to receive a personal letter from the company's founder. It helps cement the positive relationship between the company and customers.

The Letter Dear ______:

Thank you for your very complimentary letter regarding Davidson and Greerly's environmental policy.

When we decided to eliminate all nonbiodegradable packaging 16 months ago, we did so because we believed that our company had a responsibility to the environment. Over this period we have been gratified to see other companies and our customers become more involved in this vital initiative. We know that in a small way, we are making a contribution to the survival of our planet.

Your letter is significant to us. It strengthens our commitment and enthusiasm, and makes all our effort worthwhile. All people like to believe that they are appreciated and we are no exception.

Thank you again for your praise. I've taken the liberty to enclose some literature on steps we all can take to make the environment safer for ourselves and the generations to come.

Sincerely,

Adam Greerly

Key Points

- Thank the customer for the compliment.
- Take the opportunity to describe the policy further, or make comments about its purpose.
- Allow customers to feel that their effort in writing the letter has special value to you.
- When appropriate, offer some additional information regarding the policy or others that may be of concern to the customer.

16.3 Recognizing an Anniversary as a Customer

Situation A customer's anniversary with your company is a perfect opportunity to recognize and reward the event, thereby maintaining goodwill and future business.

The Letter

Dear ______:

It is time for our company to celebrate our fifth anniversary together with you. It was five years ago this month that you brought your first printing job to us here at Pinnacle Peak Printers.

Since then, our relationship has grown and been mutually beneficial. We remember when you were printing your catalog only twice a year, instead of the monthly printings and mailings you are now doing. You've come a long way and we are glad to have been a part of that growth.

Please accept the enclosed coupon worth $100 towards your next print job in celebration of our anniversary together.

Sincerely,

Peter Pressman
President
Pinnacle Peak Printers

Key Points

- State the reason for the letter, and be sure to mention which anniversary you are celebrating. Your customer may be surprised to learn how long they have been with you!
- Reminisce about business when the customer first started buying from you and where they are now.
- Offer a reward—such as a plaque, cash-value coupon, or gift—to recognize the customer for this milestone.

16.4 Appreciation of a Volume of Purchases

Situation While all customers deserve excellent customer service and recognition, large volume customers require special attention. Companies should have systems in place that track customers' purchasing history. Levels of activity need to be established to alert you when milestones are reached. As customers reach these plateaus, some token of appreciation is in order.

The Letter

Dear ______:

Congratulations! Your recent visit to the New York Prestige Hotel qualifies you for FREE membership in the Prestige Platinum Guests Club for business travelers.

Since you are already a member of the Prestige Frequent Guest Club, you know that staying at a Prestige Hotel offers you excellent accommodations, first-rate service, and attractive room rates. As a Platinum Club member, you automatically are upgraded to a suite, receive complimentary breakfast and cocktails, and pay our lowest corporate rate. Plus, many other advantages unavailable to non-club members.

Please return the enclosed quick application form. Once we receive it, we will rush you your Platinum Club Card, membership kit, and a little surprise. You'll be able to take advantage of your membership privileges immediately upon receiving your card. So send in that application today!

And remember, membership in the Platinum Club is reserved solely for our best business customers who demand the finest accommodations and unequaled service. Congratulations again on your membership!

Sincerely,

Platinum Club President

Key Points

- Using enthusiasm, inform the customer of the milestone.
- Offer sincere thanks and appreciation for the customer's business.
- Make sure the customer understands the exclusivity of your offer.
- Special privileges, pricing, service, and the like can be offered to encourage the customer to respond.

16.5 For Being a Good Customer

Situation Greystone Engineering has received a contact from Butler Industries to work on a new highway project. Butler has been an excellent client for many years, and Greystone decides to write a letter to show its appreciation.

The Letter

Dear ______:

We just received your order to begin work on the Red Brook Highway project, and it reminded me of just how good a customer you have been. I thought this would be the perfect opportunity to express our appreciation for all the business you have given us over the last eight years.

But it's not only the activity of your account that means so much to us. You are truly an outstanding client. The team here agrees that you conduct business in a professional manner that makes working with you both a pleasure and a rewarding experience. Moreover, the courtesy and respect you show our staff says a great deal about the people at Butler.

Thanks again for the order. We're looking forward to working with you on this important project.

Sincerely,

President

Key Points

- State your appreciation for having such a "good" customer.
- Explain why you value the customer. If it is for more than just their business, say so.
- Make the letter as personal as possible. If the customer has been doing business with you for a long time, indicate the number of years. If there is a special relationship between personnel of the two companies, mention that.
- Close with the expectation of a positive, continuing relationship.

16.6 For Being Patient with a Difficult Situation

Situation

As it has been said, "The best laid plans of mice and men often go awry." Indeed, there are times when you do everything wrong when dealing with a customer. When customers endure such catastrophes, they must be thanked for showing patience. It is also essential to offer something—a gift, discount, premium—to show that customers are important to your company and that you want to make up for the difficult situation.

The Letter

Dear ______:

As customer service manager of Pottery by Mail, I wanted to express our appreciation for your patience and understanding with the late delivery of your flower pot order.

While delivery of our products is usually made within seven days of an order being placed, your order took almost two months. The many damaged shipments, lost shipment, and wrong color shipment must have been extremely frustrating. Your willingness to work with us through these difficulties was unusual. We are very grateful for your cooperation.

Now that you have your flower pots and the problems are behind us, we wanted to show our appreciation with the enclosed gift certificate. We know that these unusual circumstances will not happen again and that your next order will be handled in a manner that meets your expectations.

Thanks again for your willingness to work with us.

Sincerely,

Sales Manager

Key Points

- Express your thanks for the customer's understanding.
- Show that you realize how frustrating the events must have been to the customer.
- Extend your appreciation with a gift, discount, or some other token.
- Reinforce your expectation for future business.

17
Information-Gathering Letters

"What do my customers really want?" Across the nation, at companies large and small, people are asking themselves that question. For all the questioning, though, it's surprising how few take a direct route to the answers—by simply asking their customers.

Sure, there's a tendency for people to hold back, to say that everything is fine when it really isn't. But despite that inclination, there's a trend toward customers' expecting quality service and appreciating interest in their plans, wants, and needs from the companies they do business with.

You may want to develop a survey or questionnaire to be mailed to all customers, or handed out at the time of purchase or at a trade show or exhibition. Phone calls to a sampling of customers may seem more appropriate for your particular product or service—or for the type of information you need. Or a more open-ended letter asking for customer feedback may work for you. In all cases, it is vital to make it easy for your customers to respond, to let them know how much you value the information they have shared, and to make them know that you plan to act on it!

Whichever method you choose to gather information, remember that you have a relationship with your customers. What could be more natural than saying to a relation, "I care about you and want to do my best for you. What could I be doing better?"

Therefore, if you really want to know what your customers think, what plans they have for the next year, and how you could better satisfy them, just ask!

Key Points

- Customers who expect quality service will understand and appreciate your efforts to acquire information from them.
- If you've created a relationship with your customer, it will seem natural for you to stay in contact and ask for the information you need to do a better job for them.
- While no effort to gather information will ever get a 100-percent response, if your information-gathering letter is well-written and makes it easy for the customer to respond, you should be able to obtain plenty of valuable information. As an added bonus, you'll also show the customer that you really care.

17.1 Letter Requesting Information About Upcoming Buying Needs

Situation Universal Galleries provides wall art to institutions such as hotels, restaurants, and offices through decorators and decorating services. While they are always commissioning new work, the quantity of pieces and types of work ordered depend on their customers' needs. To better meet those needs, they send the following letter to all customers.

The Letter Dear Mr. Maxwell:

We're very pleased to have been able to meet your needs for wall art during the past year. From contemporary to traditional, abstract to representational, watercolors to oils, fabric hangings to posters, we're constantly searching for new pieces to provide you with exactly the look you want for your clients.

And now we're asking you to help us do an even better job for you. How? By letting us know whatever you can about your expected buying needs for the next year.

In the space below, please fill in whatever you anticipate purchasing for clients during the upcoming 12 months. If you are able to project quantity, let us know that. If you're only able to make a guesstimate, that's fine too. And if all you can tell us is that the new Inn you're working with is leaning towards a Southwestern motif, fill that in.

Universal Galleries is exploring new product sources and will put this information immediately to work to serve you better.

A return envelope is enclosed for your reply. Thanks so much for your help.

Sincerely,

President

Key Points

- Remind the customer of the products or services you provide.
- Ask the customer for help, and explain how the information you're requesting will be used.
- Be specific about what you've asked the customer to do for you. Make it as easy as possible to respond.
- Thank your customer for the assistance.

17.2 Letter Requesting Information About a Buyer's Patronage of Competitors and Their Products

Situation Overnight Courier is relatively new to the overnight delivery industry. To find out more about their customers' buying habits and why they lose sales to competitors, they send the following letter to their customers.

The Letter

Dear ________:

Do you remember the days before overnight delivery? If it was Monday night and you had to get that document to Seattle by Tuesday morning, there was nothing you could do, short of flying it there yourself.

But today a variety of rapid delivery companies are able to provide you with many of the services you need—though perhaps not all of them.

Overnight Courier would like to be your single source for *all* your quick delivery needs.

We know which services we currently provide for you. Are there other services you are currently getting from our competitors—or even some you need but are unable to find?

In order for us to provide you with more of what you want, we need your help. The information you can supply on your current overnight delivery requirements will enable us to develop more of the services you want at pricing you can afford.

I've enclosed a brief survey and reply envelope for your response. We look forward to hearing from you and appreciate your assistance.

Sincerely,

President

Key Points

- Set the stage for your survey by mentioning the type of services your company provides for the customer.
- Let customers know you are aware that they also buy from your competitors.
- Explain what you plan to do with the information you've requested on the customer's buying habits. Make sure to include ways the customer will ultimately benefit.
- Tell customers what you want them to do next.
- Express your appreciation for the information.

17.3 Letters Requesting Friends as Referral Names

Situation Mark Harrison is a house painter who acquires much of his new work through referrals from satisfied customers. In addition to asking for a referral when a job is completed, Mark sends out a customer letter six months to a year after finishing a job to see if the homeowner has any friends or neighbors who might need his services. The letter not only generates names of prospective clients but keeps Marks's name in the minds of his past customers.

The Letter Dear Mr. and Mrs. Wagner:

I hope you're as pleased with the way your home looks today as you were when I finished painting it earlier this year.

As a matter of fact, I've had several occasions to show the photographs you allowed me to take as a good example of how the look of a home can change with the use of color.

You may remember that at the time I finished painting, you referred me to the Minettas. I'm scheduled to do work for them in April, and I want to again thank you for the referral.

As a business that offers a personal service to homeowners, nothing is more important to me than a referral from a satisfied customer. Do you have any other names you would be willing to give me as possible painting prospects? If you can think of a friend or neighbor who might currently be in the market for a house painter who still believes that the customer deserves the highest-quality work possible for a fair price, I'd appreciate your giving me their names.

I've enclosed a self-addressed stamped envelope for your convenience. Or you can call me at 314-555-8200 anytime.

Thank you in advance for your consideration.

Sincerely,

Mark Harrison

Key Points

- Remind your customers how satisfied they were with your work.
- Reestablish your connection by bringing up an event or conversation that occurred between you and your customer.
- If there have been earlier referrals, thank the customer for the past assistance.
- Ask for a referral. You may also want to note some of the benefits of doing business with you or your company.
- Tell the customer exactly how to respond—and make it as easy as possible to do so.
- Thank customers in advance for their assistance.

17.4 Letter Requesting Co-workers as Referral Names

Situation *Nursing Today* is a monthly trade magazine for registered nurses who provide their services outside the hospital staff structure. To obtain the names of potential new subscribers, the circulation department sends a letter to all current readers requesting the names of co-workers as possible referrals.

The Letter Dear ______:

Would you like to help your co-workers learn more about the issues most important to today's registered nurses?

Key issues like

- How to set and get the fee levels you deserve.
- The three most important nursing trends for the '90s.
- How to make sure your employers put state-of-the-art protective measures in place for their health professionals.

Nursing Today—your access to everything that's vital and new for the nursing practitioner—will be sent FREE for two months to any co-workers and associates whose names you give us.

And we'll give *you* one additional FREE month on your current subscription for every qualified referral name you send us—up to five names.

So do your fellow workers a favor—and you'll do yourself one too—by filling out the referral form below.

Sincerely,

Subscriptions Manager

Key Points

- Ask your customers to do something that will benefit their co-workers and associates.
- Remind customers how their co-workers will benefit by receiving your product or service.
- Tell your customers what you will do with any referral names you receive.
- Offer something special to customers for assisting you.
- Add a final reminder that the customer will be doing these co-workers a favor by referring them.

17.5 Letter Asking How Satisfied a Customer Is with the Company's Service

Situation Washmaster Leasing Corporation leases laundromat appliances. To check on customer satisfaction and the likelihood of lease renewal, Washmaster surveys customers during the year.

The Letter Dear ______:

According to our records, Main Street Laundromat has requested six service calls for the 20 machines on your lease contract since March 1.

Because we strive to make the name Washmaster synonymous with the highest-quality service in this business, it is important for us to know that you are satisfied with our efforts. If not, what can we do to satisfy you? How else can we maintain Washmaster's 25-year reputation for premium customer care?

Please help us provide you with better service by responding to the following questions on the back of this letter. It should take only a few minutes of your time.

How satisfied have you been with Washmaster's service? (You may answer from 1 to 10, with 10 being the highest.)

If you are not entirely satisfied, how can we serve you better?

Based on how you feel right now, would you renew your lease with Washmaster on March 1?

Again, thank you for your time and effort. Your feedback and suggestions are very important to us.

Sincerely,

President

Key Points

- Establish your current relationship with the customer and explain why you are writing the letter.
- Ask for the information you need.
- Explain that the information is really for the customer's benefit.
- Thank customers and tell them how much you value their help.

17.6 Letter Requesting Information About Business Expansion Plans

Situation Chandler Design specializes in space planning and decorating services for professional offices. A letter is sent to all customers from the previous five years to find out about their upcoming expansion plans and to renew Chandler's connection with inactive customers.

The Letter

Dear ______:

In August, 19____, we completed work for you on the remodeling of your Gable Street office and I remember how proud you and your partners were of the results. I hope these past two years at 7 Gable Street have brought you much success.

Chandler Design has grown too since 19____. We've increased our design staff, added an office art and accessories group, and created a department for office electronics recommendations.

These additions evolved from our efforts to meet customers' needs. To continue our efforts, it would help us to know if you are planning any office expansion or additional remodeling within the next year. Do you foresee any special requirements as part of these plans? Now that you've had an opportunity to live with your new offices for awhile, are there any services we could have provided during the remodeling process that would have made the results even better?

Your answers to these questions will be greatly appreciated. A form and reply envelope have been enclosed for your convenience.

Thank you.

Sincerely,

Key Points

- Refresh your customer's memory about your past relationship and the customer's satisfaction with your work.
- State how your company has improved since the customer last worked with you and how customers' needs influenced those changes.
- Ask your customer for the information you want.
- Express your appreciation for the customer's help. Make it easy to respond.

bs

18

Questionnaires and Surveys

There's no mystery about which companies will be successful in the future. Companies that will grow and prosper in this decade and into the twenty-first century will be those that understand what their customers want and then deliver those products and services quickly and cost-effectively.

No better investment can be made in the future of one's company than sending surveys and questionnaires to customers. These information-gathering documents are snapshots of customers' views of your company, and they offer an insightful look at where the company should be heading.

Questionnaires and surveys should be written by marketing professionals who understand the science of information collection. But even if you create your own in-house version, the findings will be enlightening.

There are some simple steps to follow when writing a questionnaire or survey.

1. Decide on the information you are seeking and make sure your questions will secure that data. Test all questionnaires on employees and customers before they are sent out, to verify that they are easy to

understand and that the responses answer the questions you want answered.

2. Design the questionnaire or survey so that the reader will find it inviting to complete, with simple instructions and straightforward questions.

3. Formats for questions that have proven successful include open-ended questions, fill in the blanks, and ranking scales. The idea is to have the respondent be able to complete the survey with little effort.

4. Make it easy for the reader to respond. Include a self-addressed stamped envelope so that the form can be returned without cost to the customer. Preprint the respondent's name and address on the form when possible, and offer a gift as a token of your appreciation.

Many companies experience a return rate on questionnaires and surveys as low as 5 percent. Providing an incentive to the reader and designing the survey to be effortless can increase the return rate dramatically.

Key Points

- Questionnaires and surveys can provide valuable information. Use them frequently.
- Carefully write questions that will provide the needed information.
- Make the instructions and format as simple as you can.
- Provide an incentive to the customer for responding.

18.1 Cover Letter for a Questionnaire

Situation No one likes to complete questionnaires. Therefore, your request must immediately appeal to the customer in a positive way. One approach is to simply ask for a favor. Whatever the approach, customers need to be shown the benefit of spending their time answering your questions. Naturally, the tone of the letter must be friendly and informal. A form letter proposal will end up in the waste basket.

The Letter Dear ______:

May I ask a favor of you?

As a loyal Artco customer, you are probably aware of the emphasis we put on customer satisfaction.

To learn exactly how customers like you feel about our products and services, we periodically send questionnaires to find out what you really think about us.

We understand how busy you are—and that filling out a questionnaire is probably the last thing you'd like to do today—so we made ours as quick and easy as possible. It should only take you a few minutes, and there's a handy postage-paid return envelope for your convenience.

Thank you in advance for your help. We're dedicated to improving the way we do business—for our customer's benefit.

Sincerely,

General Manager

P.S.: Last year our customers' suggestions resulted in free alterations. Who knows what great ideas you'll suggest this time?

Key Points

- Immediately explain the reason you are writing. Ask for a favor.
- Describe how the questionnaire helps you better serve the customer.
- Make completing the questionnaire seem easy.
- Thank customers in advance for their assistance.

18.2 Thank You for Returning the Questionnaire

Situation People who respond to your questionnaire deserve special credit. They have gone out of their way to be helpful—probably because they really like doing business with you and want to feel like part of the family. Offer these people an enthusiastic thank you. Where possible, a small gift or discount certificate reinforces your appreciation.

The Letter Dear ______:

Thank you!

We received your completed questionnaire and want to express our gratitude for the time and effort you took to help us.

The information that you and other customers have provided will help us better serve you in the future.

As a token of our appreciation, we are enclosing a certificate for a free lunch at Garfield's—our in-store cafe. Next time you shop at Rubin's, lunch is on us!

Thanks again for your assistance.

Sincerely,

General Manager

Key Points

- Offer an enthusiastic thank you.
- Tell customers how they will ultimately benefit from this.
- When it is appropriate, offer a small token of appreciation.
- Close by thanking the customer again.

18.3 Questionnaire About Customers' Product Needs

Situation To survive in today's competitive market, it is especially important that new products are developed only when a customer need or interest has been established. This skin care products company sends a customer needs questionnaire to all recent buyers with the intention of learning more about the customer's product wants and interests.

The Letter Dear ______:

There's a Free Gift from Body Smooth Waiting for You!

Thank you for your recent purchase from Body Smooth's Lotions line. By now, you may already be noticing a difference in how your skin looks and feels.

Remember that all our products have a 100-percent Customer Satisfaction Guarantee. Plus, skilled skin counselors are available at every Body Smooth Shop to help you choose the products that are just right for you and your skin needs.

To help us continue to develop the skin products you want most, please tell us more about your skin concerns and product needs. A self-addressed, stamped envelope is enclosed for your convenience.

Your response is very important to us!

Sincerely,

President

P.S.: If you include your name and address with your questionnaire, we'll send you a special Body Smooth gift to say "Thanks!"

The accompanying questionnaire appears on the next page.)

BODY SMOOTH QUESTIONNAIRE

1. I have purchased the following Body Smooth Items:
   (See product list enclosed.)

   ______________________ ______________________
   ______________________ ______________________
   ______________________ ______________________
   ______________________ ______________________

(Please grade each of these products based on your personal experience—A, B, C, or D. An "A" is the highest grade possible; D is the lowest.)

2. I have never purchased the following Body Smooth products, but would like to try them in the future:

   ______________________ ______________________
   ______________________ ______________________

Is there a particular reason(s) why you have not yet purchased these? ____
____

3. Assuming high quality and reasonable pricing, I would also be interested in purchasing the following if they were added to Body Smooth's product line: ______________________________________
   ____
   ____

Send my Body Smooth gift to: ______________________
____
____

Key Points

- Open with an attention-getting offer that will entice the reader.
- Identify customer as buyers and thank them for their patronage
- Explain why you are asking them to complete the survey
- Reemphasize the gift in the P.S.

18.4 Questionnaire About Customers' Service Needs

Situation Double A Auto Repair asks for customer feedback on their service capabilities through the following letter/questionnaire.

The Letter Dear Mr. Mason:

We're proud to have Mel's Limousines as a Double A Auto repair customer and want to continue to satisfy you with our mechanical expertise and attention to customer needs.

This month, we are conducting an evaluation of our service department and need your feedback. Please take a few minutes of your time to answer the questions below. Only your input can help us best serve our customers.

Thank you.

Sincerely,

Owner

QUESTIONNAIRE

1. Which Double A Auto Repair services have you used in the past year?
   ______
2. On a scale from 1 to 10 (with 10 the highest), how satisfied have you been with:
   The quality of our service? ______
   The cost of service? ______
   The friendliness of our service people? ______
   The ease of scheduling appointments? ______
   Other? ______
3. Are there any services you would like us to provide that are currently unavailable? ______
   ______
4. Are there any services now available that you feel should be changed?
   ______

How would you change them?

5. Have you been entirely pleased with our service staff? ______

If not, do you have any specific recommendations? ______

______

Please share any other comments for our service evaluation: ______

______

______

______

Key Points

- Immediately establish the customer's special relationship with you.
- Tell the customer why you are asking for feedback.
- Keep your questions brief and to the point.
- Whenever you can, include questions that can be answered by a single word or grade.
- You may also want customer suggestions. Leave enough space for an adequate answer but not so much that the customer feels you're asking for a long or time-consuming response.
- Provide space for other comments in case customers have something they want to share. You can often get valuable data this way.

18.5 Evaluation Form

Situation Gooding and Mercott Brokerage offers one-day seminars to stimulate business. Although the program does not openly sell to the attendees, it does offer solutions to customer problems that tie into opportunities available through G&M. A closing evaluation form requests reactions to the program and the customer's interest in the investment opportunities available through G&M.

The Letter Thank you for attending today's seminar, *Economic and Financial Trends of the Uncertain Nineties*. Gooding & Mercott Financial Services appreciates your participation.

Because we want our seminar programs to better meet your information needs, please complete this form before you leave today.

1. What is your overall evaluation of today's program? (Circle one.)
   Excellent   Good   Satisfactory   Fair   Unsatisfactory
2. Which parts of today's seminar were most helpful to you? ____________
   ____
   ____
3. What additional areas would you like to see covered in future programs?
   ____
4. Was the material presented more or less what you expected?
   Yes   No
   How did it differ from your expectations? ____________
   ____
5. How would you rate today's speaker? (Circle One)
   Excellent   Good   Satisfactory   Fair   Unsatisfactory
6. Would you like Gooding & Mercott to send you additional information on any of these investment opportunities mentioned today? (Circle all applicable.)

   Funds   Unit Trusts   Tax Frees   Stocks   Bonds
7. We would like to include your comments in our next brochure. Limit your comments to the space provided. ____________
   ____
   ____
   ____

Please sign below to give Gooding & Mercott permission to use your comments in future brochures and promotional materials.

____
Signature Title

____
Company Name

____

Key Points

- Thank the customer for attending.
- State why you want this information.
- Ask for the customer's overall reaction to your program and the person(s) representing your company.
- Ask customers what they liked best and what could have made the day even better.
- Find out if your program was what they expected, that is, if you provided what you promised.
- Use the questionnaire to further qualify your customers on their interest in the products/services you can provide.
- Take advantage of this opportunity to request customer testimonials. Make sure to get the customer's signature allowing you to use the testimonial for promotional purposes.

18.6 Trade Show Attendee Questionnaire to Be Distributed Prior to the Show

Situation Datacomp, an exhibitor in the upcoming Info Mart show, is having a cocktail reception for customers and prospects. They use the invitation to their reception to also find out about customers' familiarity with and interest in a new Datacomp product.

The Letter Dear Customer:

We're looking forward to seeing you at Chicago's Info Mart, June 6–10, Booth 2340 on the main floor.

In fact, we're writing to you now to invite you to Datacomp's Gala Reception on Tuesday night, 6 P.M., right after the close of business. An RSVP card and a series of questions are attached, which we would appreciate your mailing back to us in the enclosed envelope.

Please take a few minutes of your time to answer the following questions.

I plan to attend the Info Mart show next month and visit Datacomp's booth to see their new System 2000. (Yes) (No)

My company is already familiar with the System 2000 technology and wants to hear how we can benefit from its use. (Yes) (No)

We have no current need for this new technology but will stop by Datacomp's booth anyway. (Yes) (No)

I plan to attend Datacomp's Reception on Tuesday, June 7.

(Yes) (No) and expect to bring ________guests.

We hope to see you in Chicago!

Thank you for your cooperation.

Key Points

- Tie your questions in the customer's response to your invitation.
- Let customers know you appreciate their response and have made it easy by enclosing a reply envelope.
- Keep your questions as short and to-the-point as possible.
- Information requested should tie directly into your trade show exhibit.
- Thank the customer for cooperating.

18.7 Trade Show Attendee Survey to Be Distributed at the Booth

Situation 21st Century Sound Systems is a stereo equipment manufacturer. At the annual industry trade show, customers are asked to provide information about buying preferences through a short survey. As an incentive, respondents will be entered in a drawing for a new product being introduced at the show.

The Letter

Just Two Minutes of Your Time Will Give You a Chance to Win a New 21st Century 2000 Portable Sound System

We know just how hectic a trade show can be! But just two minutes of your time to fill out the answers requested below will enter you in a special drawing for your own 21st Century 2000 Portable Sound System. And we'll know more about the kinds of products you would like to see developed by 21st Century Sound Systems.

Thank you for your time. If you're our winner, you'll be notified by mail and phone at the completion of this show, on Sunday, October 5. Good luck!

1. Which products have you purchased from 21st Century? ________
   ____
2. Which models have been most popular with your customers? ________
   ____
3. Are you satisfied with the quality of 21st Century Sound Systems' products? ________________________________
4. Do you feel our products offer good value for the price? ________
5. What additional products would you like to see us offer? ________
   ____
6. Are you already able to purchase these items from other manufacturers?
7. Are there any aspects of buying from 21st Century Sound Systems that you feel could be improved? ________________________________
   ____

____

Thank you for your help!

Good luck in the 21st Century Sound Systems Drawing!

Key Points

- Trade shows can be very demanding. Offer your customer an incentive for answering your survey.
- State why you need the information.
- Let customers know you appreciate their help.
- Tell customers the rules of the drawing and wish them good luck.

18.8 End-of-Year Questionnaire About Satisfaction with Supplier

Situation The Renard Foundation is a special interest publisher serving the medical community. To start the new year, they mail a customer survey to find out more about how satisfied their customers are and what can be done to improve customer relations.

The Letter

We need your help!

Dear Friend:

We hope you had a Happy and Healthy New Year and wish you the best for 19____!

As we start the new year, we would like to ask you a small favor. So that we can serve you better, please complete this survey and return it to us in the enclosed envelope. Your answers will be reviewed by our Board of Directors, and your feedback will be instrumental in helping our company develop the best possible products while providing the type of customer service you desire.

Thank you for your assistance.

Please complete:

1. What did you order during the past year from The Renard Foundation? ____booklets ____activity books ____videos ____slide programs ____coloring books ____other
2. How are you using the products that you ordered? ____________________
3. How was the quality? ____________________
4. How was the delivery? ____________________
5. How was the customer service? ____________________
6. Was the price fair? ____________________
7. What other products or titles would you like to see us develop? ____________________
8. Do you have any other suggestions that would make your purchasing from The Renard Foundation a more satisfactory experience? ____________________

Name (Optional) ____________________ Title ____________________
Organization ____
Address ____
City ________________ State ________________ Zip ________
Phone ____________________

Please return to: The Renard Foundation, 730 5th Avenue, Dover City, New Hampshire, or send in the enclosed envelope.

Key Points

- Tell customers you need their help.
- Tie the New Year into your request for customer feedback.
- Let the customer know what you plan to do with the information.
- Thank the customer for helping you.

18.9 Survey of Perception and Use of Competitors and Their Products

Situation *Manufacturing Today* is one of several publications for top executives in manufacturing and operations management. To determine which publications are being read and purchased by prospective readers and customers, *Manufacturing Today* sends out a survey under the name of an independent research firm. A cover letter mails with the survey.

The Letter Dear ______:

Will you please help us?

We've been asked to conduct a survey to find out your perception of editorial publications in your industry. It is very important for us to know what you, as an industry leader, consider most important in business publications and how the existing publications meet your criteria.

Just a few minutes of your time to fill out the questions on the next page will help provide you with more of the information you really want and need.

A postage-paid reply envelope is enclosed for your convenience, and all returns are confidential.

Thank you for your assistance.

Sincerely,

Director of Research

(The accompanying questionnaire appears on the next page.)

QUESTIONNAIRE

1. Are you involved in manufacturing management for your company?
   (Yes) (No)
2. What is your job title? ______________________
3. Do you rely on trade publications for manufacturing news, trends, and product information?
   (Yes) (No)
4. Rate the magazines below based on your satisfaction with each to provide the specified information—5 is the highest rating. Mark NI if unfamiliar with the publication or its quality in a particular area.

	Overall Editorial Content	*New Product Information*	*Industry News*
Manufacturing Today			
Manufacturing News			
Operations Management			

5. What kind(s) of information is most important to you in a trade publication? ______________________
6. What do you feel is lacking in these or other industry publications? What would you like to see more of . . . or less of? ______________________
7. If you could only receive one trade publication, which would it be and why? ______________________

Thank you for your cooperation.

Key Points *In Your Cover Letter*

- Ask the customer to help you.
- Let the customer know the purpose of your survey.
- Tell customers how they will benefit from providing this information.
- Make responding as easy as possible. Reassure the customer that the information provided will be confidential.
- Thank the customer for responding.

In Your Questionnaire

- Make sure you're reaching the right person.
- Whether you're preparing the questionnaire in-house or with outside market research assistance, carefully think through the information you want to obtain and which questions will provide this information.
- Keep your questions as brief and to-the-point as possible.
- Always thank the customer for participating.

19

Payment and Return Policy Letters

Letters about customer payments and returns are a common part of the day-to-day workings of any business. Some customers pay too much, others not enough. Payments get lost in the mail, and returned merchandise needs to be acknowledged. These are just a few of the types of situations that regularly arise between buyers and sellers.

Often, a company considers these customer service functions to be routine matters to be assigned to an appropriate clerk. Yet no interaction with your customer is purely routine. Each provides an opportunity to resell yourself and strengthen your company-customer connection. You can make a difference by consistently using these circumstances to create the best customer relationships possible.

Make doing business with your company as easy as possible by accurately including all the specifics of the situation within your letters—dates, invoice numbers, dollar amounts, and other information. Even if you are responding to a customer who has that information on hand, putting all the facts right in the text of your letter is always helpful. Provide reply envelopes, employee names with phone numbers, and anything else that your customer may need to reply. If you have existing paperwork that pertains to the situation, attach a copy with your correspondence.

While the importance of a prompt customer reply should be obvious, it is surprising how many businesses feel that several weeks to reply to a customer is satisfactory. The quicker the reply to your customer, the more concerned you'll appear with their satisfaction.

Be brief and straightforward in your correspondence. Keep in mind, though, that you have a relationship with the customer that can be enhanced by the tone of your letter.

When there is a dispute, avoid accusations and always look for a resolution that is fair to all parties.

Remember that the mechanics of these exchanges may seem to require little effort, but by responding professionally, promptly, and personally, you can do much to reinforce your other customer service efforts.

Key Points

- Expect your business to provide plenty of opportunities for correspondence regarding payments and returns.
- Use these opportunities to strengthen customer relations rather than simply treating them as routine matters.
- Make it as easy for customers to do business with you.
- Promptness counts!
- In any sort of conflict, avoid making accusations or assigning blame.
- Even the way your company handles a routine customer return affects your company-customer relationship.

19.1 Overpayment Letter, Balance Enclosed

Situation Often companies make errors in paying invoices. When an overpayment is made, a quick response to the customer shows your good faith and helps build customer loyalty.

The Letter Dear ______:

Thank you for your payment of invoice #2343. Your check #00123 for $678.54 represents an overpayment of $24.45.

We have enclosed our check #121112 for the above amount. As of this date there is no outstanding balance on your account.

We appreciate your continued business.

Sincerely,

Manager

Key Points

- Help the customer understand the situation by stating the check numbers and amounts involved.
- Enclose a refund rather than a credit if possible.
- Thank the customer for the business.

19.2 Overpayment Letter, Balance Held as Credit

Situation Many companies handle overpayments with credit memos. The advantage, of course, is that the money stays with the company until the customer places a new order. If that is your company's policy, the customer should be given the option to request an immediate refund. The following letter takes that approach.

The Letter Dear ______:

Thank you for your check #090, in payment of invoice #958. Your payment of $32,987 represented a $1700 overpayment. As you can see from the attached invoice, you were entitled to a quantity discount on product #A56, which you did not take.

Enclosed is our credit memo #00678 for $1700. You can apply this toward future purchases or request a refund check. However you wish this matter to be handled, we will be pleased to assist you.

We at Adams Supply Company want you to know that we appreciate your consistent business over the last five years.

Sincerely,

Manager

Key Points

- State the number and amounts of the invoices and checks involved.
- Offer the customer a choice of credit memo or refund.
- Thank customer for their loyalty.

19.3 Underpayment Letter, Remit Balance

Situation Intentionally or by accident, customers sometimes submit a partial payment rather than payment in full. It is important for the company receiving an incomplete payment to let the customer know right away that money is still due.

The Letter Dear ______:

Thank you for your September 13 payment of $139.43. As you can see from the enclosed statement, there is still a balance of $100.00 due on your account.

Since our invoices are payable upon receipt, we'd appreciate your prompt payment for the outstanding balance. A reply envelope has been enclosed for your convenience.

Any questions regarding billing can be directed to our Accounts Receivable Department, Ext. 435.

We appreciate your attention to this matter.

Sincerely,

Enc.

Key Points

- Thank the customer for the payment made and state that there is a remaining balance. Include a statement or other paperwork for reference.
- Restate your terms or the specifics of the customer's past-due account status.
- Ask for payment. You can make it clear that the balance is due now in a direct but polite way.
- Make it easy for the customer to respond by enclosing a reply envelope.
- Provide appropriate contact information if the customer wishes to speak to a company representative.
- In closing, express your appreciation in advance for prompt payment.

19.4 Underpayment Letter, Discount in Jeopardy

Situation Because of an incomplete payment, a customer no longer qualifies for a special discount. The supplier must now explain this to the customer and request the balance due. Two ways to handle this type of situation are suggested in the following letter.

The Letter

Dear ______:

Thank you for your check #676 for $789 in payment of invoice #000213.

Unfortunately, your payment did not satisfy the invoice, and $600 is outstanding.

As you know, you received a 20-percent discount on your order, and this was reflected in invoice #000213. As explained on your invoice, discounts apply to orders that are paid in full within 30 days. Because we are now past that payment period and your account still has an open balance, we cannot offer the discount. Therefore, a new invoice is enclosed without a discount.

We are sorry we cannot honor the discount past the 30-day period. As you can understand, it is offered as an incentive to customers to make prompt payments.

Sincerely,

Manager

Key Points

- Thank the customer for the payment, citing the related account, invoice, and check numbers.
- State the amount of underpayment.
- Refer to the discount policy. Tell customers exactly what you expect and what they must do. Use one of the two options provided.
- Make it easy for the customer to respond by enclosing a new invoice and, when possible, a business reply envelope.

Option The third paragraph can be replaced with a more lenient policy: If you remit the outstanding balance within 10 days, we will honor the 20-percent discount. After 10 days, however, we will expect payment of the balance plus the 20-percent.

19.5 Late Payment Letter

Situation By keeping on top of receivables, a company can greatly reduce bad debts and delinquencies. A reminder letter should be sent once a customer's payment is overdue. By being alert to the payment status, and reacting quickly, your collection problems will be greatly lessened.

The Letter Dear ______:

As of today, we have not received payment on our invoice #00023 for $1201.

You are aware that your lease payment is due on the 15th of each month and that payments received after that date incur a late penalty of $32.

Since you have always made your payments on time, we are extending the payment period by ten days. Please mail your payment for $1201 to the above address today in order to maintain your excellent payment record and avoid a late penalty charge.

Sincerely,

Manager

Key Points

- Explain the situation by making specific references to invoice numbers.
- Do not threaten or bully.
- Remind the customer of your payment terms.
- If the customer has had a good payment history, offer a grace period if possible.
- Emphasize that, by paying on time, customers will not jeopardize their good credit record and avoid a penalty.

19.6 Check Not Signed

Situation It's surprising how many payment checks are received unsigned. Since this oversight occurs so frequently, your company should have a ready-to-go response letter available. It pays off as both a convenience and time saver.

The Letter

Dear ______:

We have received your check #768, in payment of invoice #021987. Unfortunately, the check was not signed.

We are returning it to you for signature. For your convenience, a postage-paid business reply envelope is enclosed.

Thank you for your prompt payment.

Sincerely,

Manager

Key Points

- A brief, straightforward letter is needed in this situation.
- Offer a postage-paid business reply envelope to ensure a prompt response.
- Thank customers in advance for their payment.

19.7 Invalid Credit Card Number

Situation Order takers and customers often make errors in transcribing credit card numbers. Upon discovery of an invalid number, a letter should be sent to capture the correct information. The letter must be sent out immediately, while the customer is still in a buying frame of mind. A delay could lose the order.

The Letter Dear ______:

Thank you for your book order.

Unfortunately, we cannot process this order because the credit card number given us is invalid.

Possibly we have made an error in capturing your number. The number that we have is #____________. If this is incorrect, please indicate the correct number here: #____________.

Or if you would like to give us another credit card number, you can do so in the space below:

____MC ____VISA ____AMEX ____DINERS

Card #____________

We apologize if we have made an error.

Please return this letter to us today, so that we can rush you your order.

Thanks again for your interest and assistance.

Sincerely,

Manager

P.S.: I've enclosed some information on three newly published books that you may want for your library.

Key Points

- Provide the invalid number to purchasers and ask them to correct it.
- Allow the buyer to give another credit card number. Do not insult the customer with references to "bad" cards or other insinuations about their creditworthiness.
- Since the customer is in a buying mood, offer additional products that may be of particular interest.

19.8 Expired Credit Card

Situation

Frequently customers who charge their order to a credit card are unaware that the card has expired. Upon discovery of this problem, the supplier should immediately send a letter informing the customer of the credit card's status and asking for either a valid credit card or another means of payment.

The Letter

Dear ______:

In processing your order and billing it to your credit card #__________, we were informed that the credit card has expired.

If you have received a new number or would like to charge your order on another credit card, please complete the following:

____MC ____VISA ____AMEX ____DINERS

Card Number:__________

Expiration Date: __________

Signature: ________________

The amount of your current order is _______. This includes shipping and handling.

You can also pay for your order by enclosing a check or money order.

Please return this letter today so that we can rush you your order. A postage-paid, business reply envelope is enclosed for your convenience.

Sincerely,

Manager

Key Points

- Inform the customer about the expired credit card, and cite the card's number for reference.
- Ask for a new credit card number, check, or money order.
- Help the customer by offering the convenience of a postage-paid return envelope.

19.9 Billing Adjustment: Extended Terms

Situation Good customers deserve special treatment—especially in a difficult economic climate. When Crawly Pavement Company places a very large cement order, they ask A&J Supply for an extra 30 days to pay. A letter is sent granting the extended terms after A&J's credit department reviews Crawly's payment record.

The Letter Dear ______:

Thank you for your letter of November 10 requesting extended payment terms on your order #PB213.

After reviewing your credit history, the accounting department is pleased to be able to grant you 60-day billing.

Because of the unusual size of the order and your excellent payment history, your request was approved. We do, however, want you to understand that 30-day terms are our regular terms, and they will be in effect on future orders.

Thank you for the increased business you have given us over the past year. We hope we have been of service in granting you your request.

Sincerely,

Manager

Key Points

- Inform the customer that the request for extended terms has been granted.
- Explain why the decision was positive.
- Note any restrictions or conditions.
- Thank the customer for the business.

19.10 No Record of Payment Received

Situation Customer promises for payment need to be diligently followed up. In this case, a promised check never arrived. By quickly contacting the customer, the accounts receivable representative can keep control of the outstanding account and expedite payment.

The Letter Dear ______:

We are writing regarding our outstanding invoice #45634 for $345.00. When we spoke on May 9, you told me that your check #0023, had been issued and mailed.

It is now over a week since our conversation, and we have not received your payment.

Please put a stop on check #45634 and send us a new check by overnight mail. Your prompt attention to this will prevent a late payment penalty and protect your good credit status.

Thank you for your assistance.

Sincerely,

Manager

Key Points

- State the reason for the letter. Note the previous conversation.
- Avoid accusations. Express your concern over the outstanding balance.
- Provide a means for immediate satisfaction of the invoice.
- Let the customer know that, by answering your request immediately, credit problems will be averted.

19.11 No Record of Merchandise Returned

Situation Nonreceipt of returned merchandise is a common problem. It affects both distribution and accounting, and requires immediate resolution. A letter firmly stating the company's policy is in order.

The Letter Dear ______:

In your letter of September 12, you indicated that you were not paying our invoice #3421 since you were returning the merchandise from your order #AS90.

As of this date, we have not received the merchandise, and therefore are unable to credit your account. Invoice #3421 is outstanding in the amount of $3100.

If you have returned the merchandise, please have your shipper provide us with a tracer showing delivery and a signature from our receiving department. If the order was lost in shipment, we are not responsible and you'll need to settle with the shipper. In any case, the open invoice must be resolved.

Please call me personally if you have any questions. We look forward to clearing up this matter promptly.

Sincerely,

Manager

Key Points

- State the reason for your letter, with specific reference to the invoice number or order number.
- Explain your company policy.
- Tell the customer what you expect to be done.
- Suggest that the customer call you personally with questions.

19.12 Acknowledgment of Returned Merchandise

Situation When merchandise is returned, an immediate acknowledgment is due the customer. By responding quickly, you show the customer that your operation runs efficiently. Additionally, you show your concern for the customer and build confidence in your operation. The bottom-line benefit of an efficient return ackowledgment policy is future business with the customer.

The Letter

Dear ________:

We have received your return of your order #7869 for 12 dozen Ming Tea Pots. We are sorry that this merchandise did not meet your expectations. A credit memo is enclosed that cancels our invoice #542.

Also enclosed is a brochure describing our new line of oriental place settings. All tableware pictured is hand-crafted in Thailand, and offers unusual decorative value. We are sure that you will want to display these items in your store this fall.

Again, we are sorry about the tea pot order. We look forward to working with you this fall season.

Sincerely,

Returns Department Manager

Key Points

- Acknowledge the return.
- Make reference to the order and invoice numbers.
- Express your regret that the customer was not satisfied.
- Use the opportunity to present related or new products.

19.13 Statement of Return Policy Letter

Situation Quick Express Company ordered software from Information Systems, Inc. Unfortunately, the software did not perform the needed tasks, and the buyer wishes to return the merchandise. In response to a letter asking for return instructions, Information Systems sends this letter explaining their return policy. It is Information Systems' intention to make the return as simple and trouble-free as possible.

The Letter

Dear ______:

I am sorry to hear that you would like to return your recent order.

As you know, Information Systems, Inc. wants its customers to be completely satisfied with their software purchases. Everything we sell is offered on an unconditional, 30-day guarantee. Therefore, we are happy to accept your return and provide you with a full refund or credit.

Here is how our return policy works. Simply call our returns department at 800-555-5555. Have the invoice number from the upper left corner of your packing slip handy. We'll give you a return authorization number and shipping address. The return shipping cost will be paid by Information Systems. In cases in which we are exchanging merchandise, we can arrange a pick-up and delivery at the same time.

Pack your merchandise in its original shipping container, and enclose the return authorization number with your shipment. Upon receipt of the merchandise, a refund check or credit to your charge card will be issued immediately.

Again, we are sorry that you were not satisfied with your purchase. We hope that you find our return procedure easy and convenient. We look forward to working with you again.

Sincerely,

Manager-Returns Department

Key Points

- Tell customers that you are sorry they were not satisfied with the merchandise ordered.
- Explain your return policy.
- If possible, absorb all costs for the return.
- Let the customer know that you are trying to take the trouble out of returning orders.
- Express your regrets again, and reinforce the expectation of future business.

19.14 Letter Offering Discount for Early Payment

Situation To encourage speedy customer payment, a special discount for payment made within a specific period that is shorter than the usual payment terms may be offered. The following letter is an example.

The Letter Dear ______:

I have just learned of your order #4739 for 24 gross of nylon piping.

We would like to thank you for this large order. We know you will be satisfied with the excellent quality of the merchandise and the low price due to our quantity discounts.

I thought you might be interested in learning how you can save an additional 5 percent. Our usual terms are net 30 days. However, for this month only, orders paid within 7 days of invoice date will receive an added 5-percent discount.

To take advantage of these added savings, act today.

Sincerely,

Accounting Department

P.S.: We have enclosed a copy of your invoice for your convenience. Make your payment now and save an additional 5 percent.

Key Points

- Acknowledge the customer's order.
- Present the special discount for fast payment.
- Tell the customer what to do to take advantage of this offer.
- Use a P.S. to reinforce the savings.

19.15 Response to Refusal to Pay Due to Lack of Satisfaction with a Product

Situation A customer's lack of satisfaction with a product needs to be handled carefully. It is rare that a company can force a customer to keep an unwanted product. And, if you were to succeed, the customer would surely never order again from the company. In this case, an important customer is unhappy. Even though the order was custom-produced, the company must prove to the customer that its satisfaction is the most important consideration. This is accomplished by crediting the invoice and reproducing the order.

The Letter Dear ______:

I have been notified by the Accounting Department that you have refused to make payment on our invoice #896 for custom-sized shipping containers. I understand that you spoke to Jane Johnson and explained that you are not satisfied with the quality of the folds on the boxes.

After reviewing your customer history, I realize that you are an excellent and long-standing customer. Over the past seven years, you have purchased shipping materials on numerous occasions and have never returned an order. Therefore, it is obvious to me that the problem is in the manufacturing.

I apologize for any inconvenience that this situation has caused you. If you wish, we will be happy to run the order again and make sure that the products meet your quality specifications. In addition, we will run an extra 5000 containers and send them to you at no cost.

We'll issue a pick-up order and have our trucking company bring back the 20,000 containers that are not satisfactory.

Of course, we realize that this problem has put you behind schedule, so we'll rush the new order to you within 10 days.

I hope this arrangement is satisfactory. We really appreciate the business you've given us over the years and want to continue to work with you.

Please discard invoice #896. If you have any questions, I can be reached at my direct line, 555-5678.

Sincerely,

Jake Robbinson
Customer Service Manager

Key Points

- Show the customer that you are familiar with the details of the problem.
- Apologize for the trouble that the customer has experienced.
- Let customers know that you consider them valued patrons.
- Provide a solution that the customer will appreciate.
- Include your phone number so that the customer can discuss any unresolved issues directly with you.
- While your resolution to a problem must be appropriate to your company's particular products and services, ask yourself if it would be more cost-effective to find a new customer or satisfy the existing one.

19.16 Acknowledging a Refund Due to Defective Merchandise

Situation A customer has returned a recently purchased helium pump. Upon inspection, the seller has found the merchandise to be defective, and now needs to let the customer know that a refund is forthcoming.

The Letter Dear ______:

A refund check in the amount of $179.95 is being processed and will be sent to you by the first of the month.

We regret that the Balloons Galore Helium Pump did not perform for you as promised. Our Service Department did find a valve system defect that caused the problem.

If you are interested in a trial purchase of another Model T24 or any of our other helium pumps, we would be happy to offer you a 30-day trial purchase period prior to billing and our standard 100-percent Customer Satisfaction Guarantee.

Please accept our apologies for any inconvenience we have caused you. We hope you will give us future opportunities to show you the usual high performance of our products.

Sincerely,

Key Points

- Open by letting the customer know how soon the refund check will be sent and the exact amount.
- Accept responsibility for the defective product, and state the nature of problem if the information is available.
- Remind the customer of your guarantee policy and any other assurances you can give to promote customer confidence for future purchases.
- While you may not be able to compensate for customer inconvenience, you can make the refund process as easy as possible.
- Close by offering apologies for the problem, and leaving the door open for future business.

20

Claims and Adjustment Letters

Customer claims and the related adjustments are regular parts of any business. While it may not always be possible to adjust a claim exactly as requested, a company is always able to:

- Respond promptly to a claim.
- Let customers know you are taking their claims seriously.
- Resolve the claim immediately or tell customers the matter will be investigated promptly.
- Offer special accommodations to customers while the claims are being looked into.
- Be specific about how long the resolution may take.
- Extend your apologies for inconveniencing the customer.

In whatever way a claim is ultimately resolved, you will want to do everything in your power to prevent this simple business matter from turning into something more detrimental to your relationship. Quick action, sincere concern, and a dedication to customer satisfaction will go a long way toward making sure this does not happen.

Key Points

- Always respond promptly to a customer claim.
- Let the customer know right away what your records indicate and, if there is a difference of opinion, what you plan to do.
- Give the customer your time frame for resolving the claim.
- Use the customer service opportunity to show your concern for your customer and your ability to provide a satisfactory resolution.

20.1 Acknowledgment of a Claim Letter

Situation A customer claims an overcharge on an order. The company must acknowledge this claim and tell the customer how it will be handled.

The Letter Dear ______:

Your letter claiming an overcharge of $293.43 on order #3058, received on April 8, has been turned over to our Central Accounting Office.

Please allow four to six weeks for disposition of your claim. In the meantime, you may disregard any invoices for this order.

Thank you for your patience.

Sincerely,

Manager, Store #43

Key Points

- Acknowledge the customer's claim, including the specifics provided.
- Tell the customer what you have done with this claim.
- Let the customer know how long your response will take.
- If special instructions are needed about how to handle business in the meantime, offer it in the letter.
- Thank customers for their patience while you resolve the claim.

20.2 Acknowledgment of a Claim Letter with Further Investigation Needed

Situation A customer responds to an invoice by claiming that the account has already been paid in full. The company must acknowledge the claim, let the customer know that it will be checked into further, and be clear about how long it will take to resolve the matter.

The Letter Dear ______:

We are in receipt of your letter of October 15 stating that your account has been paid in full as of August 30.

Since our records show a $79.67 balance, we will need to review this matter further. Please allow four weeks for our findings.

In the meantime, no interest will be charged on the disputed amount.

Sincerely,

Accounting Department

Key Points

- Start by acknowledging receipt of the customer's claim.
- State your company's current position on the claim.
- Let the customer know how long it will take you to investigate.
- If interest is usually charged on an outstanding balance, tell the customer how this is to be handled during this period.

20.3 Acknowledgment of a "Short" Order, Bill to Be Adjusted

Situation A customer receives 11 of 12 cases of latex gloves ordered, and contacts the supplier to find out about the remaining case, along with the need for an adjusted bill. A prompt supplier response is important to satisfy the customer.

The Letter Dear ______:

Thank you for letting us know that your PO #735 delivered on June 25 contained 11 cases of T2 latex gloves rather than the 12 cases ordered.

Our stock shortage was not discovered until the merchandise was being loaded on the truck, and the packer neglected to adjust your packing slip. Our internal paperwork, however, has been adjusted and a corrected invoice is already being processed.

Please forgive any inconvenience this has caused you.

Additional stock of the T2 glove is expected this week. Unless I hear otherwise, one carton will be shipped and billed to you as soon as possible. Of course, there will be no delivery charge for completion of your order.

We appreciate your patience in this matter.

Sincerely,

Key Points

- Thank the customer for notifying you about the "short" order.
- Offer a simple explanation.
- Let the customer know that you have already taken steps to adjust the bill.
- Apologize for the inconvenience.
- State how you plan to complete the original order. Make this as easy as possible for the customer.
- Express your appreciation for their understanding or patience.

20.4 Acknowledgment of "Short" Order, Balance to Be Reshipped

Situation A supplier must reply to a customer regarding partial delivery of crystal vases for a chain of gift shops.

The Letter

Dear ______:

I'm sorry that we were unable to deliver your complete order of crystalware this month. I understand that you did not receive six of the items ordered on your PO #9056.

When inspection was made prior to shipment, we found that those items were damaged. Replacement stock has been ordered and is expected by the end of this month. Unless I hear from you otherwise, the six items will be delivered to you on November 5. You may hold payment until the order is completed.

I hope this will be satisfactory. Your patience and understanding are appreciated.

Sincerely,

Key Points

- Apologize for the incomplete delivery. State the specifics involved.
- Briefly explain the cause.
- Tell the customer what you have done to replace these items and when they will be reshipped.
- Let the customer know how to handle payment.
- Express your desire to satisfy the customer and your appreciation of his or her understanding.

21

Controversial or Politically Sensitive Issue Letters

Probably no letter is more difficult for a company to write than a response to a customer's demand for information on a controversial or political issue.

Many companies do not answer these requests at all. Others try to respond in a manner that will not offend or excite either side. Still other companies answer these questions in as responsible and truthful a way as possible.

Companies that answer their customers' most sensitive questions create a valuable dialogue between the public and the company. While some may disagree with the company's policy, the exchange and open communication will earn mutual respect.

We've decided to use actual company letters in this chapter since fabricated letters on invented issues might only confuse the reader.

The examples chosen are letters regarding environmental policies—a subject on many consumers' minds today—and one to which most companies will need to respond sooner or later.

You'll notice that the three letters in this chapter are all mailed with additional environmental information. Because many environmental issues are complicated, company policies should be supported by additional data whenever possible. The extra material helps the company explain its position and assists the customer in learning more about the issues involved.

BEN & JERRY'S®

VERMONT'S FINEST ALL NATURAL ICE CREAM™

Route 100, P.O. Box 240, Waterbury, Vermont 05676 (802) 244-5641

May 22, 1991

Customer Name
Customer Address
City, ST 00000

Dear

Thank you for your letter. We appreciate the opportunity to respond to your concerns regarding our packaging.

Currently, the FDA has not approved recycled or unbleached paper for direct contact with food items, which is the main reason we do not use it for our pints. Even when/if it gains approval, chances are it will still need to be coated to prevent the pints from becoming soggy. Our current pint containers will degrade in a compost pile or in water (tearing them into pieces speeds the process). Unfortunately, they do leave a thin plastic residue due to the coating.

The whole issue of packaging is a difficult one for a company like ours. We very much wish to find alternative packaging materials which are more sensitive to the environment yet which will also protect the high quality of our products. We have been working on alternative packaging for our Brownie Bars and Peace Pops. The support tray for our Brownie Bars is now being made of 100% recycled plastic, and we eventually hope to use a cardboard support made of recycled paper in place of the tray or perhaps eliminate a support altogether, though a final decision has not been made. The outer box will be made of recycled newsprint (our Peace Pop boxes are already being made of recycled paper). We were also testing cellulose wrappers, used with our Brownie Bars, for their stability at the sub-zero temperatures needed to store our product. Unfortunately, they did not hold up, and we will be looking for another alternative to replace the plastic wrappers on the individual sandwiches.

In addition to our packaging research, we have instituted some aggressive recycling programs in both our office and manufacturing areas, and we are working in cooperation with other companies to build a market for recycled products. Because many of the changes we wish to implement require major alterations to equipment and, in some cases, the development of new materials, some of these changes will be a long time in coming. Someday, however, we hope to use and produce only recycled or recyclable products in all aspects of our business. Thank you again for your concern in writing to us; we hope to have solutions in the future which are beneficial to all.

Best wishes,

Consumer Affairs

enc: environmental fact sheet and article

We Support

1% FOR PEACE

100% recycled paper

BEN & JERRY'S®

VERMONT'S FINEST ALL NATURAL ICE CREAM™

Route 100, PO Box 240, Waterbury, Vermont 05676 (802) 244-5641

Date

Name
Address
City, ST

Dear :

Thank you for your letter. We appreciate the opportunity to respond to your concerns about the humane treatment of animals on dairy farms.

All of our milk and cream comes from the St Albans Cooperative, owned by dairy farmers in Franklin County, Vermont. Fortunately, the topography and climate of Vermont do not lend themselves to "factory farming," in which cows are confined in feed lots year-round. Cows are pastured during the spring and summer months, fed hay grown on the place, and the fertilizer is for the most part organic. These are relatively small family farms, struggling to survive in an era when "get big or get out" appears to be the prevailing wisdom.

We support Vermont family farms, believing that their independence and relatively small herd size are more conducive to human, animal and environmental health than are huge, impersonal absentee-owned farms typified by agribusiness. Our opposition to bovine growth hormone (BGH), literature about which is enclosed, is based on our concern that its use threatens the survival of family farms. We do not necessarily condone all of the practices of modern dairying, such as separating veal calves at birth and continuous breeding back for maximum milk production; however, we do recognize the need of farms to be economically viable. We are discussing working with Vermont farmers to develop a source of organic dairy products, and we believe that strengthening the organic farm movement will have a favorable impact on just such issues as you are concerned about.

Unfortunately, unlike the Holsteins that supply our milk, these issues are not black and white. We understand your concern, and we appreciate your taking the time to write.

Sincerely,

Consumer Affairs
Enc: BGH packet, position paper on federal dairy policy

We Support 1% FOR PEACE

100% recycled paper

MARY KAY

September 20, 1990

«first» «last»
«address»
«city» «state» «zip»

Dear «first»:

Thank you for your interest in Mary Kay's corporate recycling efforts. You will be glad to know that Mary Kay is on the leading edge of today's environmental crisis. I am enclosing a company fact sheet on recycling that should address most of your concerns and questions about Mary Kay's role in helping preserve our fragile environment.

Please don't hesitate to call or write again if you have additional questions or need more information.

Sincerely,

Corporate Public Relations

Enclosure

Controversial and politically sensitive letters should be:

- *Friendly in tone.*
- *Factual.* Opinions must be supported by information, statistics, and data.
- *Honest.* If you are going to respond, tell it like it is.
- *Direct.* Answer the question quickly. Build your credibility.
- *Respectful.* Treat writers, even if they disagree with your position, as individuals who deserve a full, objective answer.

The two companies whose letters we've selected for this important chapter are known to most Americans. Anyone who loves good ice cream is familiar with Ben & Jerry's of Vermont. And who is unaware of Mary Kay Cosmetics, Inc., their excellent product line, beauty consultants, and pink Cadillacs. We'd like to thank them for allowing us to reprint their letters on environmental issues.

22
Miscellaneous Letters

In addition to the more than 200 model letters we've provided so far, some situations require a letter that do not fall into any of our existing categories. We've included a few examples in this chapter.

No matter what the topic, though, your letter should always look and sound professional, projecting your company's image in a positive, relationship-building manner.

22.1 Request for Testimonial from a Satisfied Customer

Situation Satisfied customers of Elegante Catering Hall are asked for written testimonials to be used in promoting the hall's services.

The Letter Dear _______:

When you chose Elegante for your anniversary party, we promised you a perfect evening. From your guests' reactions and your praise, it appears we were successful in helping to make this a memorable occasion.

Would you do us a favor in return?

As you can probably imagine, recommendations are most important in our business. Knowing how pleased you were with your special occasion at Elegante would do more to reassure prospective clients than anything I could say to them.

I've enclosed a self-addressed stamped envelope. We would greatly appreciate your taking a few minutes of your time to help us by writing about your recent experience with us.

Thank you so much!

Sincerely,

Key Points

- Remind the customers how pleased they were with your services.
- Ask for the testimonial as a favor.
- Let the customers know how important their testimonial is to you.
- Make it easy for the customers to respond by enclosing an SASE.
- Thank the customers for their help.

22.2 Thank You for a Testimonial from a Satisfied Customer

Situation Annie Smith, a travel agent with Amberfield and Wheeler Tours, has received a very positive testimonial letter from a client. She uses her thank you letter to reinforce the customer's positive experience and encourage future business.

The Letter Dear ______:

What a wonderful letter! I can't tell you how much we appreciate your testimonial—and knowing how pleased you were with your Tuscany walking tour.

I'm glad you liked the accommodations at the Villa Romana, and I will certainly add Ristorante Speciale to my list of suggestions for future travelers.

You probably haven't even adjusted to the time difference yet, but let me know whenever you're ready to start planning your next trip. I've gotten some terrific client feedback on something I think you'll like.

Welcome back!

Annie Smith

Key Points

- Enthusiastically express your appreciation for the customer's letter and the positive feelings expressed.
- Reconnect with the customer's good feelings by bringing up one of the points from the testimonial letter.
- Let customers know you're looking forward to hearing from them again for future business.
- If appropriate, you can be upbeat and a bit more informal, reinforcing an existing and continuing relationship.

22.3 Request to Use a Name as a Reference with New Customers

Situation When asking customers to act as a reference, be sure not to make them feel uncomfortable about saying no. Some companies have specific policies against this; some individuals feel it will require time they don't have. The following sample letter illustrates a request from a small public relations firm writing to a satisfied client.

The Letter Dear ______:

May I use your name as a reference with prospective new clients?

As a valued client over the past five years, you've had the opportunity not only to work with me on a wide variety of projects, but also to see the long-term results generated by my efforts.

I will call next week for your answer. Of course, if company policy does not permit this, I understand.

Sincerely,

Key Points

- Be straightforward with your request.
- State why you are asking the customer. Include the length of time or volume of work that you've provided the customer.
- Let the customer know how you will get his or her answer.
- Give the customer a comfortable way to say no that will not negatively affect your relationship.

22.4 Customer Service Manual

An excellent way to communicate your company's customer service commitment to the entire staff is by publishing a *Customer Service Manual*. Such a document specifically states how you want customers treated and becomes an official declaration of your philosophy and procedures.

Your *Customer Service Manual* will be provided to every new employee and used as a reference whenever customer service questions arise. It ensures that all customers are treated consistently and according to company policies. The manual prevents "seat of the pants" decisions that could be harmful. Lastly, it reinforces to every employee your company's dedication to customer service excellence.

In the following manual, we have created a fictional company, Stone Publishing, for the purposes of illustration. Whether the policies and procedures statement are applicable to your operation or not, the example should prove helpful in devising a *Customer Service Manual* for your company.

Stone Publishing *Customer Service Manual*

Company Philosophy. Stone Publishing is a publisher of upscale books on the subject of design. We sell to major book chains, other publishers, and directly to the customer. Our products are of the highest quality and are priced at the high end of the market. Our niche market is small compared to other publishers. We receive 80 percent of our sales from repeat buyers. For us to continue to be successful, we must work to develop a lifetime relationship with our solid base of customers. We accomplish this by providing excellent products and superior customer service. At Stone, a satisfied customer keeps our business strong. We will do everything in our power to be responsive to our customer's needs. Every employee makes this commitment, and together we earn our reputation every day.

Statement of Customer Service Goals

- To treat every customer contact as an opportunity to build a positive relationship.
- To consider all customers as valued partners in the success of our business and theirs.
- To train all employees so that they share the company's commitment to customer satisfaction.

- To give the solution of all customer problems high priority.
- Customer callbacks should take place within one day. All replies to customer correspondence should be sent within two days of receipt.
- While all problems cannot be solved immediately, customers must be kept aware of our involvement in their solutions.
- The customer may not always be right, but the customer's satisfaction is always the goal.
- There is always an answer that can satisfy an unhappy customer. It's our job to find it!

Customer Bill of Rights for Stone Publishing

1. As a customer, you deserve to be treated with respect, honesty, and concern.
2. As a customer, you deserve to receive the best quality product for a fair market price.
3. As a customer, you deserve our products and services to live up to our advertised promises.
4. As a customer, you deserve a 30-day guarantee on all products.
5. As a customer, you deserve 48-hour delivery whenever possible. When not possible, you deserve to be notified immediately.
6. As a customer, you deserve prompt, knowledgeable answers to all your questions.
7. As a customer, you deserve the best informed Stone Publishing employee made available to you for the resolution of your concerns.
8. As a customer, you have the right to speak to the President of Stone Publishing if you are not completely satisfied with your treatment.

Customer Service Training. As part of Stone Publishing's customer service commitment, a training program has been established for all new employees. Regardless of position, department, or responsibility, everyone of us at Stone must understand and appreciate our impact on the company's relationship with the customer. A three-day training program is scheduled during the first week of each month. All new employees should speak to their supervisors to schedule attendance.

Procedures

- *Order taking:* Order takers should answer the phone within three rings and say, "Good morning (afternoon), Stone Publishing. This is Mary Evans (your name). How can I help you?" Speak clearly and cheerfully. Listen carefully to what customers want. Provide them with the information needed to place an order or to make a decision. Take special care to pronounce and spell customers' business and personal names correctly. Follow the prompts in the order entry system. You may suggest related items that the customer may be unaware of or specials from your weekly list at this point. Read back the entire order to confirm it with the customer. Thank the customer and explain when the order will be shipped.

- *Order confirmation:* A written confirmation should be sent within two days of receipt of order. For new customers, a personally written thank you note is to be enclosed. For established customers, a note thanking them for their continued business is enclosed.
- *Shipping:* We ship all orders within 48 hours of receipt. This prompt shipping policy is an important sales factor, and we insist that this time schedule be met. Special rush orders are so marked and will be shipped within 24 hours. When an item is back-ordered, the customer must be immediately notified of the delay.
- *Guarantee:* Stone Publishing offers a 30-day unconditional guarantee. Any product may be returned for any reason for full refund or credit. Refunds and credits are mailed to customers with a personalized note of concern within 72 hours of the return.
- *Returns:* Since all products are offered under our unconditional guarantee, all returns are accepted without question. A full refund or credit, including shipping costs, is mailed to customers with a personalized note of concern within 72 hours of return. Returns after the guarantee period will also be honored, although we do not promote this policy. Late returns are accepted because we have learned that forcing customers to keep products not only discourages future orders, but also increases the likelihood of nonpayment.
- *Problem solving:* Answering a customer's inquiry regarding a problem always receives high priority at Stone Publishing. Telephone inquiries are to be answered within one day of receipt; responses to written inquiries should be mailed within 48 hours of receipt. Even if a problem cannot be resolved within these time limits, customers must be informed as to what steps have been taken and when they can expect to hear from you next. Whatever the problem, customers should be made to feel confident that you are looking after their interests.
- *Claims and adjustments:* All claims must be acknowledged within 48 hours of receipt. If an immediate decision cannot be made regarding an adjustment, the customer should be notified about whatever steps are being taken and a specific date when a decision will be made. If for any reason that date cannot be met, the customer must be notified

prior to the date promised of the reasons for the delay. A new date for resolution should be specified at that time.

Credits and refunds should be expedited. If there is a delay in making such payments, the customer must be told when the refund can be expected.

- *Billing:* All billing should be accurate and timely. Errors in the billing process reflect badly on the company and can damage the relationship with the customer.
- *Collections:* While it is important to maintain an ongoing collection effort, collections personnel need to remember that they are dealing with customers and conduct themselves in a friendly, helpful manner. Under no circumstances is rude, accusatory, or threatening language acceptable.

Relationship-building customer programs. Stone Publishing has implemented several programs to strengthen the bond between the company and its customers. In addition to quality products, fair pricing, and customer care, three programs are currently in place. All employees should be familiar with the workings and benefits of each program, and be able to discuss them knowledgeably with customers.

- *Frequent Buyers' Club:* Customers earn points for purchases made and redeem them for products. Every $1000 worth of purchases earns 100 points. Customers may begin to order products with points earned once they have received 500 or more to their credit.
- *Birthday Club:* When customers place their first order with Stone Publishing, a record is made of their birthdays. Every year, one week prior to that date, a birthday card and gift dinner certificate for two is sent.
- *Anniversary Program:* Every third year, on the anniversary of the customer's first purchase, a certificate of appreciation and a gift is sent. A current list of recommended gifts is available from the Director of Customer Relations.

It's a proven fact. Companies that put their customers first, that give the customers more than they expect, and that commit all their personnel and resources to excellent service have a far better chance of success and survival in today's business climate. Make the decision now to satisfy the most important person in your business—your customer. Then step back, and watch your business flourish.

Index

About the Authors

Edward W. Werz is president of Information Publishing, Inc., a direct marketing publishing and consulting firm whose clients are a virtual who's who in the business-to-business arena. He is also publisher for The Bureau for At-Risk Youth, an educational publishing business. Mr. Werz has held a variety of key positions in marketing and product development for direct marketing and publishing companies and is the author of three business books including the bestselling *Letters That Sell*.

Sally Germain is currently director of customer services for The Bureau for At-Risk Youth, a publisher of drug prevention education and materials and other resources for youth services programs. Ms. Germain has held numerous management positions in the publishing industry with extensive experience in sales, marketing, and customer relations.